How to be a Better Deal-Closer

How to be a Better Deal-Closer

The 7Ps of Successful Deal-Closing

Simon P. Haigh

BEP BUSINESS EXPERT PRESS

How to be a Better Deal-Closer: The 7Ps of Successful Deal-Closing

First published in 2019 by
Business Expert Press, LLC
222 East 46th Street, New York, NY 10017
www.businessexpertpress.com

ISBN-13: 978-1-94784-365-3 (paperback)
ISBN-13: 978-1-94784-366-0 (e-book)

Business Expert Press Selling and Sales Force Management Collection

Collection ISSN: 2161-8909 (print)
Collection ISSN: 2161-8917 (electronic)

Cover and interior design by Exeter Premedia Services Private Ltd., Chennai, India

First edition: 2019

10 9 8 7 6 5 4 3 2 1

Printed in the United States of America.

To Margaret, Kathryn, and Alice.

Abstract

Deals are pivotal to business growth and are being struck all the time. You won't succeed in business without striking deals. Deal-closing is not limited to CEOs. To varying degrees and at different times, we all strike deals in business. Every person or organization engages in deal-closing at some point.

This book provides valuable and accessible insight into the key elements required to ensure successful deal-closing. It is written in an easy to read, no-nonsense style. It is easily accessible to those who do not know much about the subject of deal-closing. The chapters include real-life stories and insights from a wide spectrum of the author's connections and experiences.

Keywords

Deals; deal-closing; deal-making; deal-closer; negotiation; selling

Contents

Foreword

The international best-selling author or editor of 35 books including What Got You Here Won't Get You There and Triggers.

—Marshall Goldsmith

In How to be a Better Deal-closer, Simon Haigh builds on his recent e-book Dealmaking for Corporate Growth, and gives us a rich and thoroughly comprehensible framework for closing deals in business. In doing so he includes some interesting perspectives from some leading international executives, more practical examples and questions and answer sessions. It's a step-by-step guide to successful deal-closing for, as Simon says, "anyone who needs to make a deal."

What is very interesting to me is that the seven Ps Simon describes in his book are quite similar to what I teach my executive coaching clients. For instance, I teach them about the importance of listening, the importance of partnering, and one of my all-time favorites, value. Simon writes, "There is a tendency to think that a deal-closer must 'win' and the other side must 'lose.'"

As I talk about in my book *What Got You Here Won't Get You There*, one of the most rampantly bad habits among successful people is the need to win, to prove they are right, to squash the other guy into oblivion. I'll leave it to you to read more about Simon's take on creating value and fairness as it pertains to deal-closing. Suffice it to say, we are of like mind on this topic!

Here is one last piece of advice that I have for you before you venture into reading this wonderfully concise and matter-of-fact book. When it comes to deal-closing and influencing the other party (-ies) in the deal, remember that every decision is made by the person who has the power to make that decision. This will not necessarily be the "right" person, the "smartest" person, or the "best" person. If you can influence the key decision-makers involved in the deal, you can make a positive difference. If you cannot influence these decision makers, you will make much less of a difference. Once you make peace with this fact, you will become more effective at every deal you attempt to make.

Read, learn, and practice these wonderful seven Ps of deal-closing. Life is good.

Acknowledgments

A sincere "Thank You" to my wife, Margaret, and colleagues, Jeremy Balius, Celia Jordaan, and Matt Nile, for taking the time to review my original e-book Deal-making for Corporate Growth—and for being brutally honest in the process. Also, many thanks to Brian O'Kane of SuccessStore.ie for believing in this project at the very start in December 2015.

I would also like to thank Jeff and Mindi Caselden for their enduring patience in helping me develop the expertdealcloser.com e-learning tools, and particularly to Robbie Caffrey, Deva Naidu, Sean Melly, Howard Block, Dermot Mannion, Kingsley Aikins, and Gill Carrie, for building expertdealcloser.com with me.

Introduction

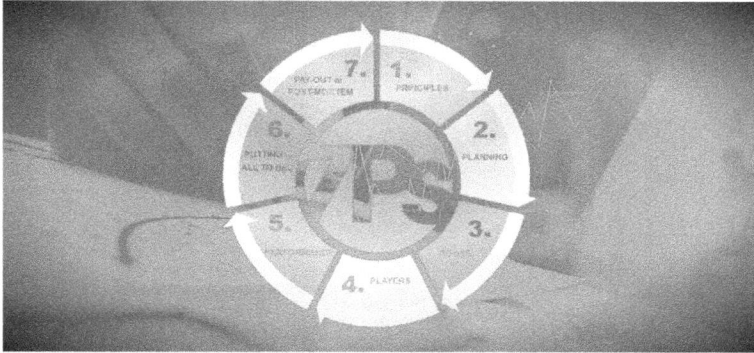

The Cambridge Business English Dictionary defines deal-making as:

The activity of making business agreements or arrangements.

Overview

Deals are pivotal to business growth and are being struck all the time. You won't succeed in business without striking deals.

The last few years have seen records set for global corporate deals. Record low interest rates in developed economies have helped to fuel a large part of this deal activity amongst all levels of companies as they have taken advantage of "cheap money" to buy, or merge with, competitors as a way to spur growth.

Worldwide mergers and acquisitions activity has exceeded $3tn for the fourth consecutive year, extending an unprecedented wave of deal making that bankers say is set to accelerate through 2018 and perhaps onwards. The total volume of deal making hit $3.5tn in 2017 (www.FT.com).

According to the Deloitte Future of the Deal Report: https://www2. deloitte.com/uk/en/pages/financial-advisory/articles/future-of-the-deal. html, while there is an urgency to spend on deals given the era of low interest rates appears to be winding down, there has also been a movement toward investing in disruptive technologies and return of private equity investors.

Deal activity in the first four months of 2018 was the highest since 2007 at $1.7tn. That was largely due to mega deals of $1bn or more that contributed nearly a third to the total deal value.

Global M&A Volume And Value

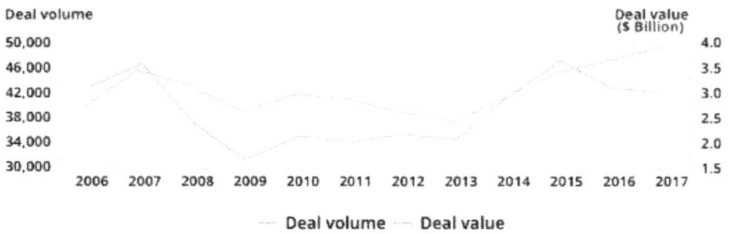

Deal volume												Deal value ($ Billion)
50,000												4.0
46,000												3.5
42,000												3.0
38,000												2.5
34,000												2.0
30,000												1.5
	2006	2007	2008	2009	2010	2011	2012	2013	2014	2015	2016	2017

— Deal volume — Deal value

Source: Deloitte Future of the Deal report   Bloomberg Quint

Mega Deal Value As % Of Total Deal Value

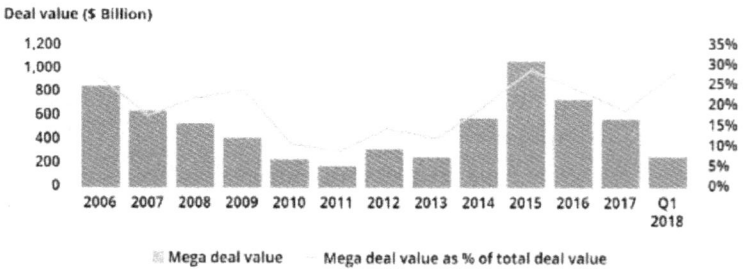

Deal value ($ Billion)

1,200													35%
1,000													30%
800													25%
600													20%
400													15%
200													10%
0													5%
													0%
	2006	2007	2008	2009	2010	2011	2012	2013	2014	2015	2016	2017	Q1 2018

▨ Mega deal value   — Mega deal value as % of total deal value

Source: Deloitte Future of the Deal report   Bloomberg Quint

Of course, this book is not just about mega-global deals and M&As, it relates to all forms of deals—from global corporate to local operational, but the same essential principles apply.

Deals and Societal Culture

While different cultures and nationalities use different methods, processes, and communication styles in deal-closing, from the beginning of time humans have been striking deals to facilitate family, trade, community, and national best interests.

Cultural differences can complicate deal negotiations and relationships in many ways. For example, words can carry different weights in different jurisdictions—in certain Asian countries, words such as "That's a problem" or "It is looking difficult" may mean that the deal discussion may well not proceed, while in certain Western jurisdictions it might be taken as a reason to reframe and move on.

In some jurisdictions, certain behaviors are viewed differently. For example, facilitation payments are considered to be illegal activity in many jurisdictions and yet in others may be considered as an inevitable aspect of "greasing the wheels" of business. Also, culture can influence the method of deal interaction. For example in the United States, a primary goal may be to get a signed deal, while in China, the ultimate aim may be more geared to establishing an effective long-term relationship.

Although cultural differences make the deal landscape even more interesting and sometimes challenging, for example deal dynamics in developing and centrally command economies can be heavily influenced by prevailing Government dynamics, the key elements that facilitate a deal—selling, persuading, negotiating, and signing a contract—are essentially the same the world over. That said, to smooth out cultural differences as much as possible, there are a number of steps that could be made such as (a) being prepared by learning up front about the opposing side and what makes them unique; (b) respecting cultural differences—do not seek to change the other side, instead, try to understand and appreciate them whilst finding ways to constructively bridge the differences; and (c) being adaptable and nimble.

Deals and Technology

Information and communication technologies such as artificial intelligence and analytics, online data rooms, and databases can enhance the deal-closing landscape. Technology and the associated increased access to precedent information for informed decision making can open up the market, reduce the power gap between parties, reduce costs by cutting out expensive middlemen, and increase the speed, efficiency, and effectiveness of the deal-closing process.

But, does technology create risk for the deal-closing process? Electronic data transmission and the use of data rooms increase the prospect of data leakage, whether through hacking, information hijacking, or newsgathering opportunism. This in turn can increase corporate costs in relation to improved data management infrastructure.

But, technology has not (yet) replaced human interaction. As we have seen, deal-closing cannot ignore human behavior. Person to person interaction is required to really draw out wants and needs and so primary and secondary issues at play in a deal scenario. Face to face discussion can also help build trust between the parties in a deal scenario which, in turn, can help to avoid conflict, disagreement, and a failed deal process.

Deals and Gender

Gender balance optimization—balancing "feminine" collaborative and emotion-led communication-based attributes with "masculine" forthright, hierarchical, and outcome-based attributes—is essential for accomplished, more sustainable, business deal negotiation. However, notwithstanding that we are all born with an instinct for negotiating deals, there is a deficit in utilizing these more feminine attributes where business deals are being negotiated. See **Annex 1** for a discussion of the importance of gender balance in negotiating deals. It first explores what is meant by negotiation and deal-closing, and then looks at why women are under-represented in negotiating business deals. It then explores why it is important to increase the participation of women and the feminine in business deal negotiation and how best to achieve this. Finally, it examines whether accessing feminine empathy and emotional intelligence can offer a potential edge in any business deal negotiation.

Deals and Generations

Deals are pivotal to corporate growth and are being struck all the time. As technology continues to advance and new business markets develop, cross-border deals will only increase.

The nature of deal-closing has undergone some paradigm shifts in keeping with the emergence of new generation of companies such as Uber, Classpass, Airbnb, Deliveroo, Netflix, Wework, Tripadvisor, and Trov. Minimal click purchasing, rapid delivery, real-time order status updates, and online feedbacks and reviews are becoming the new modern norms. How many people nowadays book restaurants and accommodation online without first checking prior online reviews?

See **Annex 2** for a discussion as to how Generations Y (or millennials), who are identified as those who were born from the 1980s to the late 1990s/early 2000s, and Generation Z, those who were born from the late 1990s/early 2000s are shaping these shifts in the nature of deal-closing.

> *Don't you dare underestimate the power of your own instinct.*
> —Businesswoman and author, Barbara Corcoran

Who Makes Deals and Why?

Deal-closing is not limited to CEOs. To varying degrees and at different times, we all strike deals in business. Every person or organization engages in deal-closing at some point. From as far back as our childhood, we possessed the innate ability to get what we want through selling and negotiating and other means—remember when you used to stamp your feet to make sure you got your own way! We are born with an instinct for deal-closing. Some people retain that deal-closing instinct and develop it as they age, while others lose it for many reasons such as social conditioning or lack of practice. And so, many of us are poorer at deal-closing and thus miss out on better outcomes.

Everyone has the potential to be a good deal-closer and it is clear that every person, organization, or nation state, needs to make deals at some point, and usually quite regularly. So, it is important to be open to a potential deal and recognize that, if you rely on your instinct, as supplemented by your experience and the skills offered by this book, you give yourself the best chance of success. Also, even if you are already an accomplished deal-closer, it is easy to slip into bad habits, so constantly calibrating where you stand in your deal-closing skills is beneficial.

Deal-closing is an active and deeply practical skill. It requires flexible and adaptable listening, reading, absorbing, and summarizing skills.

Given that selling and negotiating are innate human abilities, the premise of this book is that these, and other related, deal-closing skills can be significantly enhanced by following some proven steps. This book explains the deal-closing process in a logical, step-by-step way, and will help the reader to successfully execute business deals.

Companies around the world will continue to grow, refocus, merge—and, sometimes, retrench—through making deals. As a result, given the increasing interconnectivity—technological and otherwise—of the world's businesses, the risks of not having a good deal-closer at the helm will increase. The need for business leaders and decision-makers to be able to effectively identify a deal's strategic, financial, and operational value and then to execute and manage it efficiently will only accelerate in this ever-competitive world.

Questions

1. **How do you think deal-closing varies across different cultures?**
   Different cultures and nationalities use different methods, processes, and communication styles in deal-closing.

2. **Name some of the key elements that facilitate a deal**
   Selling, persuading, negotiating, signing a contract, and so on.

3. **Is deal-closing limited to certain people only?**
   We are born with an instinct for deal-closing and everyone has the potential to be a good deal-closer.

4. **What kind of skills does deal-closer require?**
   Deal-closing is an active and deeply practical skill. It requires flexible and adaptable listening, reading, absorbing, and summarizing skills.

https://expertdealcloser.com

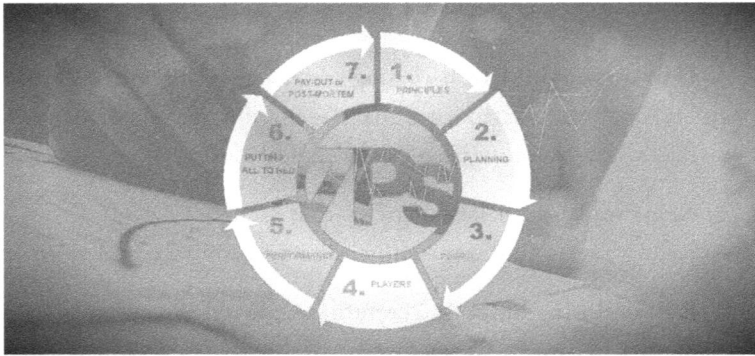

https://expertdealcloser.com

The seven Ps of successful deal-closing are:

1. **Principles**
2. **Planning**
3. **Power**
4. **Players**
5. **Performance**
6. **Putting It All to Bed**
7. **Pay-Out or Post-Mortem**

In the business world, deal-closing is clearly unavoidable. In setting out the seven Ps in an easy to follow, logical way, I have included some practical lessons I have learned, and examples from global business leaders I have worked with, over my quarter of a century making deals. This book is both an overview of deal-making for organizations and tips on better deal-closing for individuals.

Good luck with your own deals!

Simon Haigh
Dublin, Ireland, October 28, 2018

CHAPTER 1

Principles

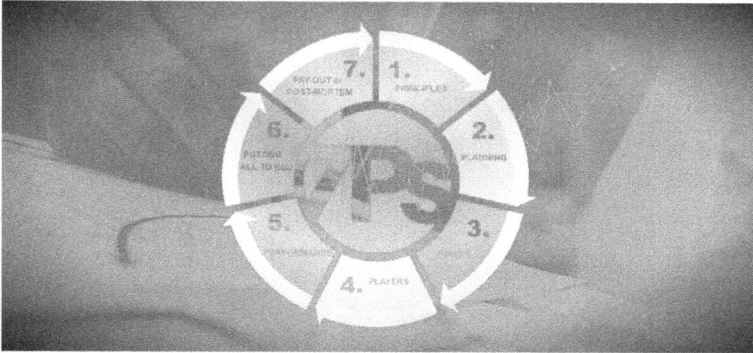

Lack of direction, not lack of time, is the problem.
—Author and motivational speaker, Zig Ziglar

This chapter covers some of the fundamentals of deal-closing before we turn to the process detail in later chapters.

Create a Clear and Simple Strategy and Do Not Rush It

Business is unpredictable, not least as macro- and micro-economic factors are always changing. Deal-closing in business is even more unpredictable, as it has its own particular set of obstacles, difficulties, and surprises that invariably arise. Ego, dubious business ethics, corrupt practices, a "head in the sand" mentality, anger, greed, and so on, add extra layers of uncertainty to the business mix. And with ever more onerous governance, compliance, taxation, legal, accounting, environmental, and corporate social responsibility factors also needing to be understood and factored into a successful deal pathway, the deal landscape soon becomes complicated.

Many things can go wrong in a deal-closing journey, such as derailing tactics from the other side, unhelpful egos amongst the stakeholders, internal or external blockages or simply that the business environment changes during the deal-closing process. Following a clear strategy, using in-depth planning, engaging the right people, ensuring stringent and exacting execution, experience, intuition, good communication skills, empathy, persistence, and constantly monitoring are all essential ingredients for ensuring successful deal-closing. You also need to be flexible and to learn from successes and mistakes in prior deals.

I have found that every deal is comprised, to a greater or lesser extent, of the same underlying principles and directions. Good deal-closers engage certain skills and techniques that maximize the chances of deal-closing success. Good deal-closers know how to play the "deal game."

Certainly, from a corporate perspective, having a clear business strategic intent for the deal in question and communicating it openly to staff is essential for obtaining their "buy-in," which in turn helps with executing the deal.

The Blocked Technology Deals

When I was a commercial lawyer for a U.S. technology multinational, twice I was tasked with handling two major technology supply deals with separate world-renowned European technology companies. Both deals had been blocked for many months.

It soon became clear to me that there was an effective stand-off between the U.S. legal team and the European based clients on each side. My investigations unravelled various reasons for this ranging from ego clashes, to cultural differences, differences of opinion and an element of deal lethargy had set in.

Have you experienced this?

What did you do?

What did I do?

To counter this, I developed a clear resolution strategy, ensured communication was as open as possible and kept an open-mind as to moving matters on.

https://expertdealcloser.com

Deal-Closing Is Broader than Selling or Negotiating

Both good selling and negotiating skills are essential components of the successful deal-closer's armory, and exist alongside other skills and techniques that a good deal-closer can call upon.

Everyone lives by selling something.
—Author, Robert Louis Stevenson

Farlex's Free Dictionary (www.thefreedictionary.com) defines selling as:

Exchanging or delivering for money or its equivalent.

Sales are the life-blood of business, driving growth, market share, and shareholder support. Selling requires skills of persuasion, which we all have in us to varying degrees from the very earliest of ages. Selling is essentially the act of persuading the other side to provide you with what you want. Remember stamping your feet to get what you wanted as a young child? Persuading, convincing and, therefore, selling are some of the most natural, familiar, and oldest of all human skills.

An accomplished salesperson can navigate the inevitable differences in objectives, drivers, viewpoints, prejudices, and even cultural differences between themselves and their customers. That said, ever-lurking to counter our innate skills of persuasion are the equally powerful human emotions and states of ego, anger, greed, ignorance and self-centeredness, any of which individually or collectively can, at any time, derail a deal. There are, however, as you will see, a number of mechanisms a good deal-closer can use to minimize these very basic, yet powerful, human factors.

Sustainable selling is not a quick fix, scatter-gun exercise. It is about empathy, doing your homework, identifying where you can help and how you can contribute. It is about listening, identifying and tracking the market and your customer needs. It is about being a valuable partner—being useful (rather than being another cost), even if that initially means saying no.

We recommend the following seven Ps for Sustainable Selling:

Plan

Understand your target audience and the problem it needs solving. Plan and research demographics, sectors, gender, age, location factors, etc., and regularly track the market. You also need to ensure you are reaching out to the right person (usually the one who holds the budget).

Pitch

Leverage first impressions. You need to show you know what you are talking about. Grab your potential customer's attention, ideally through a captivating one-liner. Use humor, if appropriate, to get attention.

Provide Value

Show that you believe in your offering. Also show that you are understanding of your customer's needs through your value proposition—the reason they should buy from you.

Personalize

Personalize your message and ensure the relevance of your unique selling proposition. Engage with your customer on an authentic, empathic level. Once you have established attention through trust you are more likely to get that all-important first meeting.

Problem-solve

Provide a tailored solution to a known need or problem of your customer through your offering. You need to have something your customer does not have and wants and/or needs. This helps trust to develop, which in turn makes it easier for customers to return and repurchase. Review and evaluate what is working and change what is not. You can use the SPIN Sales Model:

(a) **Situation**: ask the buyer to tell you what facts they need addressing;
(b) **Problem**: ask the buyer to tell you what pain they are suffering;
(c) **Implied Needs**: ask the buyer to explain the effects of the problem then propose solution(s); and
(d) **Explicit Needs Pay-off**: ask the buyer to tell you about their explicit needs and then ask them to explain the benefits your solution(s) offer.

Pursue

Think close, close close. Chase the lead within a week, otherwise you risk losing it. Always ensure meaningful activity in your sales funnel. Don't let leads dry up. Follow up every meeting. You will lose 100 percent of opportunities if you don't ask for them.

Persevere

Do not give up. Brush off rejection. Stay focused on the goal and look after yourself physically and mentally.

In sales, the seller's unique selling value proposition—the thing (whatever it may be) that differentiates the opportunity in the other side's mind from an alternative—is the key reason why the other party gives the deal-closer what he or she wants. Value propositions are a very powerful tool of persuasion. A value proposition is a definitive statement that promises, from your proposal, the delivery of value to the other side. The more specific the value proposition is the better, not least as it demonstrates to the other party that you understand what they need and/or want. More importantly, it indicates that you recognize that the deal is not just about you.

The Cambridge Dictionary Online (dictionary.cambridge.org) defines negotiating as:

To have formal discussions with someone in order to reach an agreement with them.

Note that there is no reference to money in this definition.

Negotiating is different from selling, in that negotiating requires the act of giving to receive and, in the process, it accommodates the parties' differences to facilitate an agreement.

Selling is about you establishing a need or desire in the potential buyer for what you are offering. It is then about overcoming differences through persuading the other party of the value of the service or product that you are offering. Unlike selling, negotiation necessarily requires the deal-closer to make concessions. That said, good deal-closers are able to negotiate the deal with minimal compromise.

The ability to negotiate successfully requires honed interpersonal skills for maximum success. With these skills, an accomplished negotiator can confidently ask for the outcome he or she is looking for, provided of course it is within reasonably achievable parameters. Armed with the skills of an accomplished negotiator, and provided you communicate in an effective, meaningful, and authentic way, you should not be afraid to ask for what you want in a deal. In fact, you'll be quite surprised at what you can successfully negotiate.

The types of negotiation you can use in a deal depend on the level of trust, complexity, and intention at play. Negotiations can range from:

- Simple **hustling/haggling and/or using trade-off tactics**, where the main point is to get the best price you can as quickly as possible and where there is little chance of an ongoing relationship of trust. While normally associated with more complex negotiations that involve hustling or haggling, a tactic of using trade-offs to leverage negotiation results is a tactic that can be employed, and can have the appearance of a softer form of haggling. Trade-offs allow deal parties to potentially achieve more than through a simple fixed-pie mentality compromise.

  Trade-offs replace simple "Yes" or "No" attitudes by allowing for emerging flexibility through an "I'll agree to that if you accept this important issue for me" attitude. This tactic can be made easier if multiple issues are open for discussion and an iterative process is in place to determine what is or is not of importance to each side at the same time.
- **One-off trading**.
- An **ongoing working relationship**, such as in the case of joint ventures or collaborations, where trust is critically important, as both parties need to work together over a long period of time. Usually, the complexity of the deal increases in line with the level of trust—and vice versa.

In an ongoing working relationship scenario, it is important to maintain a sustainable relationship while also keeping an eye on the challenges that may lie ahead. Rather than simply focusing on the deal itself, it is important to (a) keep one eye on the future as much as the short-medium term; (b) get to know as much as you can about the other side—their culture, direction, and relevant nuances; (c) have regular risk and deal direction check-ins to address any misunderstandings, misalignments, and loss of interest.

The heart of any negotiation usually revolves around a few key points that serve and reinforce the underlying interests of both parties; the rest of the discussion should be kept as simple as possible. A good negotiator will constantly seek to elicit the motives of the other side through questions, will seek to control the discussion, and will do everything possible to submit proposals that are favorable to him or herself.

A deal journey usually begins with selling. What then eventuates depends upon each particular situation: it could be negotiation, it could be argument, but usually it involves a back-and-forth iterative process, honing in on value for value.

Good sales people are not always good negotiators and vice versa. Each activity requires different skill sets and there are subtle timing differences to be aware of. I have seen parties come in with the negotiation part before they have persuaded or sold the other party on the deal—and then they came across as desperate or lacking substance. Conversely, selling or continuing to sell too late—for example, when you are progressed in the negotiations—can look even more desperate.

We recommend the following seven Ps for Powerful Negotiation:

Prepare
Explore the relevant issues—their relative importance, ascribed value, and what needs to be addressed.

Plan
Determine your strategy and tactics—what you need to do, what you want and consider likely negotiable ranges and relative power.

Pros and Cons
Engage in two-way discussion and information exchange. You can use the SPIN Sales Model here to determine what the other side wants through questioning and validating. It is important to build trust and rapport at this stage.

Propose

Provide tentative, conditional, suggestion(s) and/or solution(s) about how you may both proceed. If you use the SPIN Sales Model, this is where you leverage the benefits of what you are proposing to trade.

Process

Bargain with the other side so that both parties address their issues, satisfy mutual value, and make and manage any concessions.

Put It to Bed

Conclude the negotiation through a contract or equivalent format, ensuring that mutual value is captured and all agreed interests have been met.

Perform

Execute, implement, post-mortem, measure, and improve.

Value Is Key

Everything of value doesn't come with a price tag.
—Psychiatrist and counselor, Shefali Batra

There is a tendency to think that a deal-closer must "win" and the other side must "lose." If the only thing being negotiated is money, then yes, in that circumstance, a deal can be that straightforward. But I have very rarely been part of a deal scenario where money is the only factor at play. However, the goal of creating a good deal for both parties through mutual value satisfaction is not only possible, but also the only really sustainable way to do business.

While it is really important to view negotiation as deal-closing increasing the overall win-win pie for both parties, it is unfortunately human nature to default back to win-lose when issues such as time constraints, ego, conflict arise. So it is important to periodically refresh the win-win ethos throughout the deal journey by ensuring open, trusting communication and being explicit about the need for mutual win-win.

Be careful not to confuse value with fairness. Because we all have our own barometer of what is fair at any particular time, there is every chance that appealing to a higher concept of fairness when trying to conclude a deal will actually just serve to antagonize the other side.

To assist with the exchange of value, I have found it very useful to think through the deal landscape from the point of view of the other person before beginning discussions and, indeed, right the way through the deal discussion process. By doing this, you give yourself the best chance to potentially foresee the other side's "must haves" and conversely their objections, thus enabling you to better assess their value drivers.

This begs the question "How do you know what the other person will value?" The short answer is to ask them. But then don't just hear them; actually listen to the answers. A good example is recent discussions I was involved in with a motor sports team in Australia to co-produce a joint motor sports watch offering. On the watch company's side, bringing out an additional watch line was a key driver for the deal and this arrangement provided a valuable opportunity to do so. Conversely, it became clear quite early on in the negotiations with the driver's team that what was of value to them was not just a sponsorship partner but also another potential commercial avenue for their driver to pursue as he developed his options while rising through the ranks of the motor sport. Gaining an early awareness, and understanding, of each party's value drivers was very valuable in building the requisite trust for the collaboration to eventually successfully transpire. A successful deal is where both sides achieve or receive what they need.

You could use a number of value persuaders to get the other side over the deal line, particularly where it becomes clear that the other side holds something at an elevated emotional value. Taking this approach may ensure the discussion at least proceeds or, better still, that in closing the deal you achieve the needs of the other side and, in the process, create a long-term, high-value relationship.

Just as value differs from price, do not be tempted to confuse value with cost. Because something is inexpensive does not mean that it has a low value. It is important to demonstrate the value of the service or product you are offering to the other side. You should cultivate the skill of determining what a concession from you is worth to the other party. If it is of high value to the other party, a good deal-closer would usually seek to achieve something that is of high value to him or her in return. In other words, the goal is to give what is less important/less valuable to you, but more important/valuable to the other side, and to receive what is less important/valuable to the other side, but is more important/valuable to you.

Consider Alternative Pathways to Deal-Closing Success

Negotiation can be expensive and selling can be time-consuming, so it is usually wise to also consider alternative tools for making a deal.

The best alternative to a negotiated agreement (BATNA) (Roger Fisher, William Ury, and Bruce Patton introduced in their seminal book, *Getting to Yes: Negotiating Agreement Without Giving In* (Penguin 1991, second edition) can come into play here. It determines what each party has to give up or exchange to make the deal happen.

An essential element of accomplished deal-closing is to know, understand, and deal with both the best-case scenario and the worst-case scenario as the deal proceeds. In fact, it is optimal to try and determine your BATNA before deal discussions commence so that you can calibrate throughout the deal process, whether you are staying true to your positioning or getting carried away with the emotions of the deal discussions.

Knowing your BATNA, particularly if it is very much in your own interests, can then provide you with the confidence to walk away from a deal that you really should not be entering into. It is also important, in trying to get as complete a picture as possible of the other side's walk-away positions, to try and determine what the other side's BATNA is and also any gap between what they are saying and what the BATNA of the organization that they represent is.

To determine your BATNA, the question to ask yourself is "If this deal doesn't happen, what are my alternatives?" Then you should evaluate the relative value of each of the alternatives. The better the alternative(s), the less concerned you need to feel about losing the deal and so naturally the more risk you can take in the negotiation. Once you have done this, you are ready to establish your BATNA by choosing the route with the highest value to you should the current deal discussions fail. I would also suggest you create your absolute bottom line BATNA trigger value—what is the very lowest value you are prepared to run with on the current deal discussions before your BATNA is triggered?

Examples of other alternative deal pathways include:

- **Compromise**: Good deal-closers are flexible where they need to be, with a view to compromise if necessary. However, this is not the same as just agreeing to less than what you really want in order to conclude matters, which is more like capitulation.
- **Postpone and/or walk-away**: Particularly where there is deadlock, walking away can be useful in that it can provide more time to think, or to reframe the discussion so as to help bring the balance of power back to you. But it obviously is not helpful if you have strict deadlines to meet.
- **Argue**: From a positive perspective, when subtlety appears not to be working, argument can give you the opportunity to present your case, your supporting evidence and, therefore, make your substantiated point. From a negative perspective, however, argument can quickly slip into emotion and then anger, and often results in what might have been a likely deal now derailing. If the other side gets angry, just let them vent. Overall, argument, very occasionally, can be a useful tool provided time is on your side and you are patient. But use this tactic very carefully.
- **Break down a discussion into multiple components, particularly where things are not moving forward as expected or required**: By doing this, you could give yourself the chance to unclog the discussions through the making of simultaneous alternative offers with differing commercial terms, such as quality, quantity, price, contract term, and so on, and/or through trading off issues.

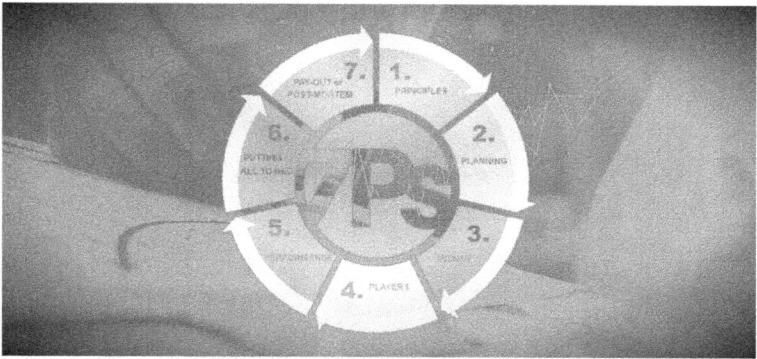

https://expertdealcloser.com

Summary

- Create a clear and simple strategy and do not rush it.
- Deal-closing is broader than negotiating or selling.
- Value is key.
- Consider alternative pathways to deal-closing success.

Executive Insights

Dermot Mannion
(Executive Coach and Mentor, Former CEO Aer Lingus and former President of Group Support Services at Emirates Airlines.)

My background is in the aviation industry, having worked in three continents, as President of Group Services of Emirates, CEO of Aer Lingus, and then more recently the Deputy Chairman on the board of directors of Royal Brunei Airlines. Also I spent four recent years on the board of one of the largest IT companies in Singapore. So as you can imagine, I have seen, come and go, quite a few deals over the years.

What are the most relevant principles you follow when creating a deal-closing strategy?

Answer:
The first thing to be said is, you need to be very meticulous in your preparations, down to every level of detail. For instance, even choosing the venue for the negotiations is very important. If you're leading the negotiations, making a statement to your team and the other side that you're going to take everybody off site for three days, let's go somewhere, let's get this deal done. That sends a very powerful statement. It also has the benefit of getting your team away from day-to-day distractions in the office, and sends a very strong message to the other side that you mean business and you mean to get the deal done.

Kingsley Aikins
(Founder and CEO of Diaspora Matters, Former Enterprise Ireland and IDA Ireland representative in Australia, Former President and CEO of Worldwide Ireland Funds and Former Chairman of LinkedFinance.)

My name is Kingsley and I've lived and worked in about six countries around the world. My background is born, educated here in Dublin, in Ireland, spent a bit of time playing rugby in France, and then got going on a proper career.

I worked for the Irish Trade Board, which now is Enterprise Ireland, and International Development Ireland (IDA); was posted to Sydney, Australia, spent eight years there. While there, I was then involved in a number of business initiatives, met a guy called Tony O'Reilly, who's a well known Irish business-person, he wanted me to run his foundation called the Ireland Funds and I ended up doing that for over 20 years. I'm now in my third act, if you know what I mean, which means I'm running a training company here in Dublin and trying to pass on some of the things that I learned over the years.

Tell me about a time where your clarity in the underlying principles surrounding a deal made achieving agreement much easier?

Answer:

I found, particularly when I was working with this philanthropic organization, raising money from individuals, particularly in the United States, that there were some key principles, I used to call it a Key Process, and if you follow this process you would have a greater chance of success than if you didn't. And that was about research, cultivation, solicitation, and stewardship.

I remember spending some time with a well known head of a film studio in the United States, actually he had a home in Ireland, and I got a chance to meet with him, and I had a terrific meeting with him, really enjoyed him. And then one day, I asked him for $5 million, which is a significant amount of money, for a breakfast. That meeting was 2.5 years after I first met him, was my 29th meeting with him, and was the first time I actually asked him to make a serious contribution. So I spent a long period of time building a relationship, which was all about building a sense of trust between us, and then we were at a right moment, a right time. If I'd gone much earlier, I certainly wouldn't have got $5 million.

Jeff Caselden

(Consultant and co-founder of Caselden Consulting, Former GM for one of Amazon's largest global development centres—Amazon Data Services Ireland Limited.)

My name is Jeff Caselden, my background has primarily been focused around about 18 years I spent with Amazon.com. I spent the majority of my time within that organization working on product search for Amazon's retail business and was the head of search for the EMEA region and was also the General Manager for their development center in Dublin, Ireland.

Tell me about a time when you failed to achieve clarity on the value that the other party was seeking and how that impacted your ability to strike a deal?

Answer:

We were developing this new product to replace an older version of a similar, less powerful product. And this product was used internally so it wasn't outwardly customer facing, so we had a little bit more leeway in terms of which to operate with in terms of product readiness. Now, I came into this situation a bit later, but from the customer's side I can definitely say that, in hindsight, while we knew what the functionality the client needed was, we didn't really have a clear sense of the value that they were trying to achieve out of using our product. So, from our own side, the primary motivator or value was in getting this product into a production use case for us, it was an important goal. Almost more as a proof of concept on the road to something greater than really understanding and meeting the needs of this individual customer. So, in the end, this resulted in a number of technical and operational issues for us as an organization, and also contributed to some severe trust issues between the two organizations as the ongoing situation transpired over the next several months.

https://expertdealcloser.com

Questions

1. **What are the types of things that can go wrong in the deal-closing process?**

   Derailing tactics from the other side, unhelpful egos amongst the stakeholders, internal or external blockages, or simply the business environment changing during the deal-closing process.

2. **What are the essential ingredients for ensuring successful deal-closing for corporate growth?**

   Following a clear strategy, using in-depth planning, ensuring stringent and exacting execution, constantly monitoring, the need to be flexible, and to learn from successes and mistakes in prior deals.

3. **What is selling?**

   Selling is essentially the act of persuading the other side to provide you with what you want. Selling is about you establishing a need or desire in the potential buyer for what you are offering. It is then about overcoming differences through persuading the other party of the value of the service or product that you are offering.

4. **What is negotiating?**

   To have formal discussions with someone in order to reach an agreement with them. Unlike selling, negotiation necessarily requires the deal-closer to make concessions.

5. **What is a BATNA?**

   It determines what each party has to give up or exchange to make the deal happen. The question to ask yourself is "If this deal doesn't happen, what is my alternative?" The better the alternative, the less concerned you need to feel about losing the deal and so naturally the more risk you can take in the negotiation.

https://expertdealcloser.com

CHAPTER 2

Planning

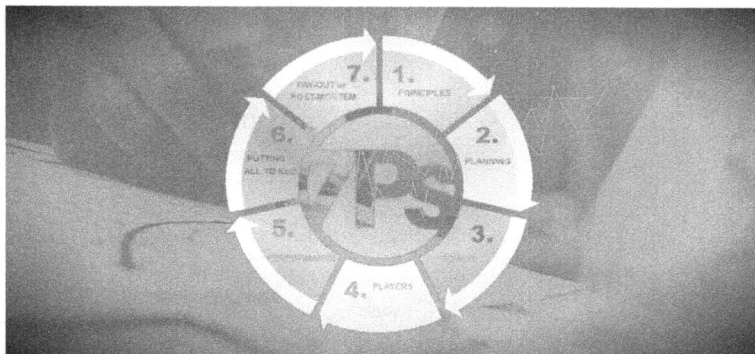

The entrance strategy is actually more important than the exit strategy.
—Businessman, Edward Lampert

This chapter will demonstrate clearly that, as in all walks of life, if you fail to plan, you plan to fail.

Thoroughly Plan Your Strategy

Thorough preparation and planning give you the best opportunity to understand all the possible strengths, weaknesses, opportunities, and threats in your deal game plan. Do not be tempted to cut corners here. Despite the temptation to do so, never rush your planning.

All successful deals begin with the right strategy, with risk analysis and measured processes in place. The tactical benefits of a well-honed strategy are that it helps you determine what you want, how you are most likely to achieve it and then to choose your optimal tools and optimal team for execution.

Speed, of course, can be important at the right time in the deal-closing proceedings, but advanced planning, clarification, and preparation are even more important. Being prepared increases your ability to success-fully get through difficulties on the deal journey with confidence. It is important to complete your preparations in advance as there may be lim-ited time to stop and regroup when you are in the thick of a deal.

Ask the Right Questions to Get the Right Answers

In my experience, the more open and authentic you are in your ques-tioning, the more you are likely to receive the quality of the informa-tion you require.

—Thomas Wedgwood (of Waterford Wedgwood fame),
Former Partner, Trestle Group and Foundation

The use of direct questions is the time-honored way of gathering informa-tion from people willing to share it, but the questioning needs to be done in a careful, measured, thoughtful way.

Face-to-face questioning also gives you the invaluable opportunity to pick up on the hints, gestures, suggestions, and other subtleties that accompany the response. After all, the whole point of asking questions is to help you explore and frame your "deal zone" (see below) for the deal and, in the process, to find out what the other side needs and wants.

I cannot overstate the importance of taking your time to suitably frame your questions. Quality answers require quality questions. Poor questions almost always result in unclear, unhelpful, vague, and time-wasting answers. Also, you will be amazed at how much confidential or sensitive information you can elicit from the other side—if you ask the right questions.

When I was a commercial lawyer, working as head of legal for Europe, Middle East, and Africa for a U.S. technology multinational, twice I was tasked with unblocking major technology supply deals with separate world-renowned European technology companies. Both deals had been blocked for many months. I decided to make site visits to these customers to determine what was causing the blockages and to find a pathway to getting the deals consummated. On-site, I used these simple tactics:

- **Once you have gathered sufficient information, asking "closed" questions** that required a "Yes" or "No" answer;

- **Using simple, direct, uncluttered language** (it wasn't always easy as a lawyer to do this!);
- **Giving the other side space in terms of time to answer**, repeating the question if necessary;
- **Waiting for the other side to answer my questions** rather than being tempted to elaborate, expand, explain, clarify, justify, or worse still, look away, to fill the awkward silences;
- **Maintaining as much eye contact** with the opposing team members as possible, particularly during the pivotal moments when I was asking questions and receiving answers;
- **Thanking the other side for each answer** provided before moving onto the next question;
- **Avoiding being interrogative or argumentative** if the other side chose not to answer or deflected the question back at me (for all sorts of reasons, some of which included confidentiality, trade secrets, and so on);
- **Being culturally astute**—for example, working with the rituals and nuances at play and particularly when it came to small talk during deal discussions. You should be attuned to appropriate cultural protocols to use these to your advantage at various stages of the deal journey.

I am pleased to say that these tactics helped me to quickly find the blockages, determine what was needed to generate forward movement and, ultimately, to unblock both deals.

You won't always be successful in eliciting the information you need from the other side—on a first try or, indeed, even after several attempts. In my experience, the other side may not answer if:

- They believe there are justifiable reasons of confidentiality, commercial or trade secrecy, or privacy (a non-disclosure agreement may be a solution here);
- They simply are not sure which information is important or relevant to provide (it's your job to make this clear to them, to avoid this situation occurring);
- They don't trust you. Perhaps they sense—or worse, have reason to believe—that your intentions are not honorable, or that you have distorted or withheld information from them.

When giving information yourself, there are a couple of important things to bear in mind:

- Never lie or fabricate information. The truth usually comes out in the end and your business reputation must always be paramount. However, do not assume the other side is not lying just because you have decided that you will not. You must probe information provided by the other side and conduct your due diligence to ensure you get as close as possible to establishing the other side's true intentions.
- Knowing which information to disclose and which to withhold requires experience, usually earned by trial and error. If you are uncomfortable (for good reason), try to avoid disclosing the information. But if you are simply trying to avoid disclosing for unjustified reasons, you will be (rightly) regarded as being obstructive or unhelpful and this will definitely not encourage the other side to be open with you (which might damage your bargaining position at a later time).

The Blocked Technology Deals

As the U.S. technology multinational lawyer, two deals that I was tasked with working on had been blocked for many months. I decided to make site visits to these customers to determine what was causing the blockages and to find a pathway to getting the deals consummated. Given what had transpired, I was confronted by a reluctance to discuss what had caused the impasse.

Have you experienced this?

What did you do?

What did I do?

To move things along, on-site with both the clients and U.S.-based parent company, I used the simple tactic of direct, authentic face-to-face questioning to build a picture of what had transpired and to then frame a strategy to move things along.

https://expertdealcloser.com

Establish the Parameters of the Deal Landscape

From a business perspective, direction-setting in relation to a deal—whether merger and acquisition, take-over or otherwise—is essential. It is critical to lay the foundations, but deal-closers should not choose generic methods to achieve their objectives. Different industries, company categories, sizes, business models, and so on all require distinct and customized approaches. Nonetheless, you must be clear on:

- **Who** you are dealing with;
- What is the **basis** for the deal;
- What are the **main issues**;
- What are the **possible outcomes**;
- What could **go right or wrong** throughout the process;
- What **risks** might arise—and when;
- What **information** you have and what is missing.

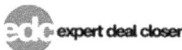

edc ● expert deal closer   **Deal Parameters**

	Record Your Deal Parameters
Who are you dealing with?	
What is the basis for the deal?	
What are the main issues?	
What are the possible outcomes?	
What could go right or wrong throughout the process?	
What risks might arise?	
What information do you have and what is missing?	

www.expertdealcloser.com

Sample Deal Parameters Chart

Only a fool would enter into a deal scenario not knowing who was on the other side, anticipating their communication style, which points to make, what the value of the exchange is to both sides, and so on. Success in deal-closing all comes down to preparation and planning.

Be Aware of Deal Location and Dynamics

There is no "one-size fits all" method for striking a deal. Similarly, there is no single best location for deal-closing. You may meet in your office, the other side's office, or on neutral ground. It can be a good idea to ask the other side where they would like to meet—if nothing else than to guage their attitude.

You usually have more control over the substance, pace, and direction of a deal discussion if it takes place on your home turf. But this is not always the case.

Generally, I find less formal settings are more conducive to small talk and thus to effective deal-closing. For example, in many countries, there is a culture of "doing business" in cafés, reflecting perhaps a more laid-back approach that leads to "good natured" business discussions. I conduct a significant amount of deal-related business in cafés, especially at the earlier, less formal, stages of a deal.

Culture and context determine the extent to which small talk is a valuable tool in the deal-closing process. You should always be attuned to what is said and, as importantly, not said. The best deal-closers are constantly alert to clues and triggers, such as how are people sitting, where are they looking, how are they looking, are drinks ordered at the start or later in the process, and so on.

Identify the Primary and Secondary Issues at Play

As part of your planning and preparation phase, it is essential to decide your key issues and priorities—for example, what your opening position and bottom line (see below) need to be and how and when to make the first move. Only then can you realistically prepare your arguments and proposals.

That said, you should resist the temptation of getting so fixated on achieving one issue that you lose sight of the relative, or potential, importance of other issues at play. Deal-closing requires an appreciation of what is important now, plus the ability to predict what will be important down the line and to balance the two.

It is essential not to rush the first step of identifying and prioritizing all relevant issues. There are essentially two types of issue at play:

- **Primary issues**: including location, size of deal, price, and so on;
- **Secondary issues**: the "nice to haves" but not essentials.

Unlike primary issues, secondary issues are rarely deal-breakers, but they can be particularly useful if there is an impasse at primary issue stage. Introducing secondary issues can add sufficient perceived—or even actual—value in the eyes of the other side to get the deal moving again. In other words, trading the secondary issues may be the means of providing both sides with the complete result they need from the deal, which they might not otherwise have appreciated.

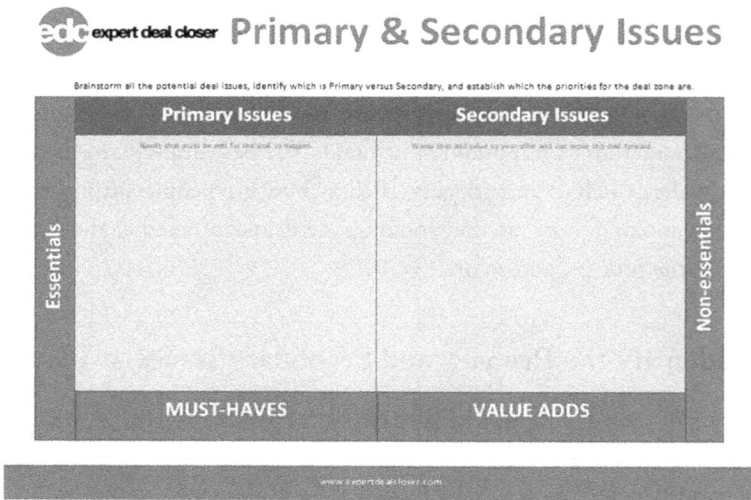

Sample Primary and Secondary Issues Chart

Distinguish Personal Wants and Business Needs

What you need and what you want aren't the same things.
—Author, Cherise Sinclair

Generally speaking, primary issues equate to needs and secondary issues to wants. A good deal-closer is able to tell the difference between personal wants and business needs, which can be important given that the latter usually must be your priority when seeking to strike a deal.

> *Results are most likely to be achieved in a deal where there is a business need.*
> —Jeremy Balius, Managing Director of OM Three Sixty

Need is usually determined by what drives the business environment. For example, the opportunity to grow and prosper is an obvious positive driver of a deal. Things become a little blurred, however, when each side views the anticipated deal trajectory in different terms. Here a good deal-closer would do all that's necessary to align the deal to maximize the growth opportunities presented.

Negative factors include threats, weakness, and problems. Counterintuitively perhaps, I find that there is nothing better than a negative push to focus the mind on a corporate deal. Nobody wants to live with negativity, so the impetus to do a deal to move out of that environment focuses minds.

While the definition, and perception, of a need can differ from person to person, it is essential to have a strategy to address the need. Use your value proposition to persuade the other side that their need(s) will be satisfied by the deal.

Develop Your Deal Zone

Once you have worked out your primary and secondary issues, you are ready to enter what I have called the "deal zone." In doing so, you must be aware that deal-closing rarely goes exactly to plan at all stages. So, just because you are organized and have categorized your issues does not mean that the other side will be able to, or even want to, differentiate between the two types of issues—and postponement or deadlock may result. Some things are just outside your control.

Before you move forward, you should check whether you have all the information that you could possibly obtain at this point and address any gaps in your knowledge. The key to the deal-closer in any deal getting what he or she wants is to provide the other side with the value they are looking for. So, you need to focus on what the other side values from their primary and secondary issues (but where the cost to you is minimized), rather than conceding too many of your own primary issues.

Developing your deal zone is really about determining how the issues at play are valued by each side and identifying the zone in which a potential deal is possible. Never assume that what is important to you is of equal importance to the other side. Never rush determining your deal zone—take time to ensure it is realistic.

To define your deal zone, you need to research, prepare, and stress-test the following positions (in order) for each of your primary (and some secondary) issues:

- **Likely outcome**: This is your realistic target to achieve;
- **Bottom line**: This is your absolute worst-case position at which you will walk away from the deal;
- **Opening position**: This is the best possible position you think you might achieve. Again, it needs to be based in reality, as you don't want to jeopardize the deal with an outlandish opening position.

The key outcome of defining your deal zone is to enable you to eventually land somewhere between your opening and likely outcomes. Be aware, however, that framing the deal zone is not a static process; rather, it is a fluid two-way process that changes and develops throughout the deal discussions.

So, as seen, the deal zone is where you set your limits by determining the likely outcome, bottom line, and opening positions for each primary (and some secondary) issue. For example, you want to obtain something for $10 but feel that you may be asked to pay $11.25, and you can't afford more than $11. In this situation, your bottom line is $11, your opening position may be $9.75 and your likely outcome may be $10.50.

edc expert deal closer

Deal Zone

Your Bottom Line	Likely Outcome	Your Opening Offer

Primary Issues	Issues that must be met in order for the deal to move forward

1.

2.

3.

4.

5.

Value Adds	Secondary issues that add value to the deal and can be beneficial to meet in order to achieve your goals

1.

2.

3.

4.

5.

www.expertdealcloser.com

Sample Deal Zone Chart

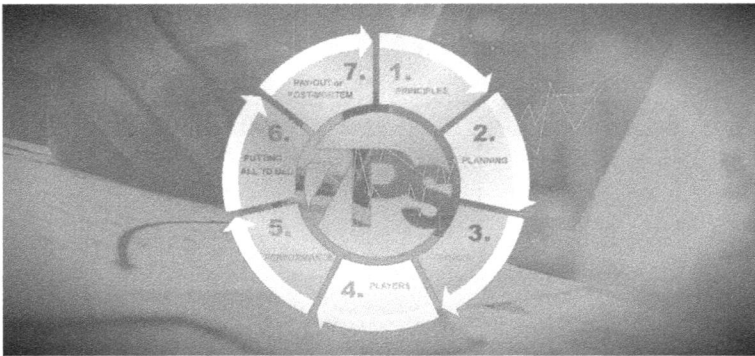

https://expertdealcloser.com

Summary

- Thoroughly plan your strategy.
- Ask the right questions to get the right answers.
- Establish the parameters of the deal landscape.
- Be aware of deal location and dynamics.
- Identify the primary and secondary issues at play.
- Distinguish personal wants and business needs.
- Develop your deal zone.

Executive Insights

Dermot Mannion

How important is it to ask the right questions to get the right answers and what can go wrong if you do not ask the right questions?

Answer:
The important thing here is, there's no such thing as a wrong question. In negotiations, people will often try to bombard you with technical terms gobbledygook, frankly. Never be afraid to stop the negotiations and say, "Look, I'm sorry, I just haven't understood what you've said. Please explain it in plain English." So, really, the key message here is, there's no such thing as a dumb question in negotiations. If it's on your mind, put it out there.

Jeff Caselden

Tell me about a time when you were able to leverage secondary issues into your favor to bring about a deal.

Answer:
Part of how this whole deal came about was through a collision of many secondary issues. While our client was generally happy enough with the product solution of ours that they were leveraging for their use, we were facing secondary issues on a few fronts so our product was constantly evolving well beyond the legacy product that our customer was reliant upon. We wanted to kill it to focus on a single product code base to make our own lives simpler going forward.

We were also trying to develop an external cloud based offering that we could actually offer as a commodity product. And lastly, we were undergoing a technical evolution within the company where everyone was moving to the cloud and away from the old ways in which we built and deployed our services. Our client was ultimately going to face a lot of the same challenges themselves, so we were able to get them to initially agree to being part of our experiment to kill all of these birds with one stone, if you will. In a sense, we were kind of offering them their own "get out of jail free" card for the technical hurdles they'd also have to resource and work through, which we were going to solve for them. I'd imagine to them it sounded like a win-win situation, they would end up with something that was cheaper, that was a more flexible option, that was a more performing product, and they'd actually get someone else to do most of the work for them.

Kingsley Aikins

Tell me about a time when you were able to leverage secondary issues into your favor to bring about a deal.

Well, you know, in the business I was working in, it was an interesting business. It was kind of a left side of the brain and the right side of the brain business. I mean, the left side of the brain wants budgets and analysis and technical issues, and the right side of the brain kind of wants purpose and meaning and all that kind of stuff, softer sort of stuff. And I found that you need to have both of those, they were the things that went together. But interestingly enough, the left side of the brain allows you to make decisions, but the right side of the brain allows you to do stuff. And I found that was an interesting kind of combination of primary and secondary sort of influences, to try and get that balance right. You know when facts come up against emotions, emotions always win. And I think we have seen that with Brexit and the election of Trump in the United States emotion always wins.

https://expertdealcloser.com

Questions

1. **What are the tactical benefits of a well-honed strategy?**
   It helps you determine what you want, how you are most likely to achieve it, and then to choose your optimal tools and optimal team for execution.

2. **Why is face-to-face questioning so important in the deal-closing process?**
   Face-to-face questioning gives you the invaluable opportunity to pick up on the hints, gestures, suggestions, and other subtleties that accompany the response. After all, the whole point of asking questions is to help you explore and frame your "deal zone" for the deal and, in the process, to find out what the other side needs and wants.

3. **What would you be foolish to enter into a deal scenario without?**
   Not knowing who is on the other side, anticipating their communication style, which points to make, what the value of the exchange is to both sides, and so on. Success in deal-making all comes down to preparation and planning.

4. **What is the difference between primary and secondary issues?**
   Primary issues equate to needs and secondary issues to wants. A good deal-closer is able to tell the difference between personal wants and business needs, which can be important given that the latter usually must be your priority when seeking to strike a deal.

5. **What are the three positions in deal-closing?**
   - Likely outcome: This is your realistic target to achieve;
   - Bottom line: This is your absolute worst-case position at which you will walk away from the deal;
   - Opening position: This is the best possible position you think you might achieve. Again, it needs to be based in reality, as you don't want to jeopardize the deal with an outlandish opening position.

https://expertdealcloser.com

CHAPTER 3

Power

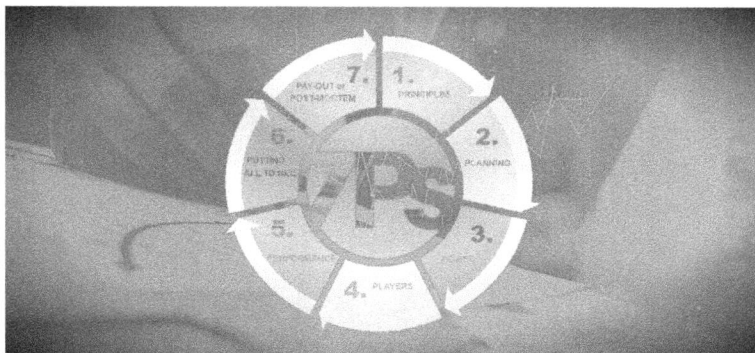

Being powerful is like being a lady. If you have to tell people you are, you aren't.

—Former UK Prime Minister, Margaret Thatcher

This chapter demonstrates the critical importance of the power balance in deal-closing and how you can ensure you have the upper hand.

The purpose of collecting so much information can only be power.
—Author and poet, Nick Drake

In a business environment, recognized types of power include:

- **Personal organizational power**: Based on a person's position within the organization's hierarchy (though be careful not to fall into the trap of believing that lower ranking staff cannot be powerful; I have come across some very powerful executive assistants). For optimal impact this should comprise a mix of not just authority but also influence.

- **Resources power**: Comprised of the breadth and depth of resources at a person's disposal (though the party with most resources at hand is not always the most powerful).
- **Shared history power**: Based on insights from prior interactions with the other party. Generally speaking, the more you know about the other side, the more you can plan and prepare your way to an effective strategy against them to optimize your deal (though, of course, this power is available to both parties). However, be mindful that it is possible to give away too much ground when you are too familiar with the other side.
- **Informational power**: Where a person has access to important or valuable information.

Information can clearly build your power. It follows that, as information underpins knowledge, converting information into knowledge produces the opportunity for even more power. Understanding the relevance and importance of information and how it can be leveraged can assist in building your power. The more you know about what is unfolding, the more you can reliably assess your position, develop your strategy, and then plan how to best execute the deal. Not only is information relevant to the inter-party dynamics, but good information management skills are also essential in corporate deals to avoid wrong decisions.

Information for information's sake is worthless: what matters is how you apply or use the information in the context of the deal. You need the right information to help you plan and execute a deal satisfactorily. Receiving valuable or meaningful information at the right time can provide you with the power to support your most important issues. This in turn can assist you to understand what the important or primary and secondary issues are for the other side. Even the act of deciding which information to provide or withhold and how best to do this can significantly enhance the dealcloser's position.

Information can be given through many methods, ranging from direct, unambiguous statements to gestures, suggestions, innuendos, and subtle hints.

One thing is for sure: a good deal-closer needs to consciously decide which information to give in order to provide maximum leverage to his or her deal. But, remember, information flow is not a one-way street. If you use information as power to compromise the other side, you will quickly find that other people stop sharing information with you—so you must use information responsibly.

Listen Deeply and Use Silence Strategically

When people talk, listen completely. Most people never listen.
—Author, Ernest Hemingway

Never underestimate the power of seeing things through the perspective of the other side in a deal in terms of your deal-closing strength. The best way to know what the other side wants is to ask them and then to actively listen to their response.

By using active listening skills, you can pick up hints, clues and other signals from body language, movements, volume and tone from which you ultimately may be able to assess the other side's positioning, likely flexibility and direction. For example, if you hear "I'm hoping for …" or "Approximately …," this weak language may suggest uncertainty and weakness. Generally, deeper and slower voices tend to project more confidence, while a variable tone is seen as more engaging than a monotone.

A good deal-closer needs to be fully present and engaged in the communication, with both body and mind actively involved. Active listening also requires you to ask questions, nod encouragement and partake in other to-and-fro activities and signals. Done the right way, you can significantly enhance your power.

Good deal-closers also use silence at strategic points in the discussion. Silence, if used the right way, can be a very powerful tool in itself. I have often found that the irresistible combination of a direct question and the subsequent discomfort of the ensuing silence can elicit an answer!

The Blocked Technology Deals

Back to the two blocked technology deals, while I was using direct, authentic face-to-face questioning to build a picture of what had transpired and to then frame a strategy to move things along I noticed some initial caginess to open up and this took quite a while to change.

Have you experienced this?

What did you do?

What did I do?

To move things along, I used active listening skills, picking up hints, clues, and other signals from what I was being told and from the other side's body language. This then helped me to assess the other side's positioning and, in turn, how to leverage a positive change in responses.

https://expertdealcloser.com

Networks and Relationships Increase Your Information Base and Deal Power

The richest people in the world look for and build networks; everyone else looks for work.

—Businessman and self-help writer, Robert Kiyosaki

The closer you get to knowing the intentions, desires, and assumptions of the other side in a deal, the more likely you are to ultimately get what you want from the deal. So, using networks and relationships is a very important additional way for deal-closers to gather the all-important information they need, which then enhances their knowledge and ultimately their power. This is particularly the case if the network or relationship connects you to the key decision-maker(s) on the other side.

In my experience, you are more likely to successfully execute business deals for a longer, more sustained period of time if you do so through relationships built upon mutual trust. How long it takes to build mutual trust depends on many variable factors.

Bear in mind, though, that close relationships are not very common in business deals. Also, relationships can sometimes get in the way if they hamper objectivity, leading to a less appropriate outcome. Being too close to the other side can skew a deal-closer's judgment in that he or she may become too focused on previous conflict or pay back some past due instead of focusing on the matter at hand—closing the current deal.

Build the Appearance and Perception of Your Power

Careful planning allows you to frame your preparations for maximum effect and maximum deal power, highlighting your potential deal strengths and weaknesses and providing you with the ability to fix any holes in your position.

As with planning, do not cut corners. As a first step, conduct a comprehensive assessment of relative power between both sides. Your relative power directly impacts your ability to execute deals. In fact, relative power is one of the most important factors that can determine the outcome of a deal.

Deal power is a frame of mind and can be developed. Even if initially it looks like there is a significant imbalance of power between you and the other side, by being smart, diligent, and measured a good deal-closer can readjust that imbalance—for example, by moving the discussion away from price to quality or some other emotive subject.

Power is not static. It usually ebbs and flows during a deal and can change sides very quickly. Whether you like it or not, your power is always influenced by your credibility, legitimacy, knowledge, authority, appearance, and influence.

Perception is an extremely powerful power source in deal-closing: perceived power can be as powerful as actual power. So focus on building the appearance (or at least the perception) of your own power.

You can create, emphasize, or reinforce your power through:

- **A SWOT (strengths, weaknesses, opportunities, and threats)**: This analysis can provide significant value in terms of identifying and improving your power-base. I regularly use this tried and tested tool with clients;

edc expert deal closer

Deal SWOT Analysis

trengths			eaknesses
• Capabilities • Competitive advantages • Resources, assets, people • Financial reserves/returns • Marketing reach • Innovative aspects • Location • Processes, systems, IT, communications • Advantages of proposition			• Lack of capabilities • Reputation, presence, reach • Timescales, deadlines, pressures • Financials • Cash-flow/-drain • Continuity, supply chain • Effects on core activities • Reliability of data, plan, project • Management cover & succession
pportunities			hreats
• Market developments • Industry or lifestyle trends • Innovation technology development • Global influence • Market dimensions, horizontal & vertical • Major contracts, tactics, surprises • Business/product development			• Political & economic effects • Legislative effects • Environmental effects • Market demand • Innovation in technologies, services, ideas • New contracts & partners • Loss of resources • Obstacles to be faced • Poor management strategies • Economic condition

www.expertdealcloser.com

Sample SWOT Analysis

- **Incentives**: The weaker your position, the more you may need to focus on offering incentives to the other side to get them over the line. The more incentives you can offer that can satisfy the other side's needs, the greater your chances of increasing your power. This is even more so when you present them as value propositions;

- **Persuasion**: Very powerful in helping you to achieve what you want, again especially if you use value propositions;
- **Alternative strategies**: The more time you spend analyzing and strategizing the costs and benefits of all the deal options, the stronger your deal position is likely to be;
- **Your networks, contacts, and relationships**: To give you significant information and therefore power;
- **Cultural awareness**: Which enables you to nimbly navigate the potential pitfalls that can arise in a deal from cultural differences.
- Finally, using a **time-out** at the right time in the deal process can give you more power. On the other hand, be careful of excessive time-outs from the other side, which may simply be a strategy adopted to avoid dealing with an issue—I have seen several deals jeopardized in this way.

Use an Agenda to Control the Discussion

Agendas are a good way of taking—and retaining—control of a discussion.

If you set and circulate an agenda in advance of a meeting, you effectively steer both the deal planning and the actual face-to-face discussion.

Agendas also help to prevent the other side suddenly changing tack without prior notice, as you have a record of what was agreed for discussion.

edc expert deal closer

Agenda

Date:	Time:	Location:

Prior Items	Items from previous meetings that require updates or further discussion

1.
2.
3.

New Items	New items to discuss

1.
2.
3.
4.
5.

Future Items	Items requiring further research or work; will be addressed in a future meeting	
Action	Owner	Date

1.
2.
3.

www.expertdealcloser.com

Sample Agenda

Use Deal Sheets to Reinforce Your Power

A deal sheet, a summary of deal discussions—is a valuable tool that provides a deal-closer not just with an ongoing record of the discussions (which is important in itself) but also with the space to stop, pause, and take stock of the progress of the deal journey. That space can be particularly useful when tempers and egos start rising.

A deal sheet is useful in terms of calibrating where the discussion is at, while also providing both sides with the ability to tweak and reframe their proposals as and when needed. Used the right way, deal sheets keep focus

expert deal closer

Deal Sheet

Date:	Time:	Location:

Item	Discussion Summary	Result/Agreement

www.expertdealcloser.com

Sample Deal Sheet

on the main issues at hand and confirm areas of agreement to date as well as outstanding action items.

They are especially useful where there are many complex, yet unrelated, issues at play. Using a deal sheet to record the progress of each separate issue is a convenient way to keep track and also to ensure that you are focusing on the right issue. Also, a deal sheet is useful in calibrating whether you are falling short in any of your proposals. By compiling a deal sheet you can see how you are doing in relation to the deal as a whole— presenting all issues in a single deal sheet enables you to see in one place the overall value of your deal, which will reinforce your power-base.

Regardless of who is taking the formal minutes of the meeting, you should ensure that you keep your own notes, made at regular intervals during the discussion. Where necessary, don't be afraid to stop the discussion to clarify your understanding of what you are recording on the deal sheet.

Organizational Cultural Robustness

Ensuring your organization itself is optimized for deal power is critically important. Some key activities that an accomplished deal-making organization can undertake include:

- Conducting effective, constantly market relevant deal-closing and/or negotiation training and follow-up support;
- Providing a collaborative, learning environment for those employees who are engaged in/involved in deal processes; and
- Monitoring deal skill development and continuous improvement.

Alan O'Neill (www.alanoneill.biz) is an internationally acclaimed change agent, speaker, columnist, and owner of Kara Change Management and has strong views about ensuring organizational cultural robustness for effective deal-closing:

The common denominator that determines the success or failure for any organization, is its culture. Vision and mission describe "why" an organization exists. Strategy outlines "what" should be done and "when." Structure details "who" will do whatever. But it is the culture that shapes "how" things will get done.

In corporate language, culture is often defined as "the way we do things around here." We can read the culture of an organization from how it interacts in the media, with customers, suppliers, and its own people. It is very encouraging to see huge brands like Disney attribute so much of their success to culture. They proactively define their culture and continue to embed it right across their organizations.

Within the definition of culture as "the way we do things around here." There is a clue. Culture in essence is a combination of the behaviors of an organization's people, the leadership style, the processes, and the rules they live by. Culture drives consistency.

A proactively defined culture impacts HR practices, engagement of an organization's people, customer experience, marketing, all kinds of decision-making and internal controls. In other words, everything that happens in an organization is shaped by its culture. This definitely includes its deal-closing capabilities.

Culture Change Tips

As Alan O'Neill continues: every organization has a culture, whether it realises it or not. The organization may not be able to define it or even have planned for it. But it does have one. There will be elements of it that are good and elements of it that are holding the organization back.

For organizations to take charge and shape their own culture for optimal deal-closing they should:

1. **Audit current culture**

   Conduct focus groups of staff, customers, and suppliers. Think carefully about what questions should be asked. Address the softer issues such as behaviors, processes, and leadership. Questions should be crafted to identify enablers and obstacles.

2. **From the findings, carefully design an independent and anonymous employee survey**

   Resist the temptation of using a generic employee survey and do not select a partner just because of the software they use. Instead, engage a company that helps to ask the right questions so that you can obtain quality insights as a result.

3. **The results may challenge the deal-closing organization**

   It is important to use the feedback and insights to design a new deal-closing culture, built on a set of values that respect the heritage of the organization's brand, the ambition of the key stakeholders, and the changes in the organization's environment (such as competition, customer changing needs, employee expectations, and so on).

Typical obstacles that emerge in culture audits include a lack of individual ownership and accountability, poor focus on customers, gaps in internal communications, inadequate internal collaboration, and disrespect for people.

Regardless of an organization's size or industry, to maximize its organizational cultural robustness for effective deal-closing it needs a culture that is relevant to its business. The devil will be in the detail.

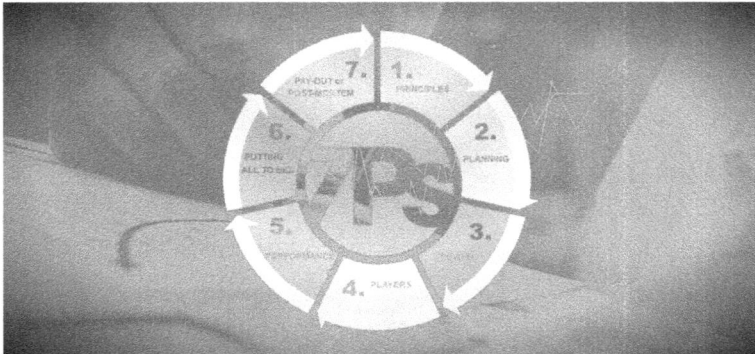

https://expertdealcloser.com

Summary

- Information and knowledge enhance your power.
- Listen deeply and use silence strategically.
- Networks and relationships increase your information base and deal power.
- Build the appearance and perception of your power.
- Use an agenda to control the discussion.
- Use deal sheets to reinforce your power.
- Organizational cultural robustness.

Executive Insights

Kingsley Aikins

Can you give me an example of how you used your network to close a deal?

Answer:
Well, perhaps I'll tell you a little story. Back in 1997, I was working for this organization which was headed up by Tony O'Reilly, a well-known Irish businessperson, who had been involved in South Africa. And in 1997, we had a difficult situation in Northern Ireland, so we arranged to bring all the leaders from Northern Ireland to South Africa to meet Nelson Mandela. Which they did and we spent three days. It was an extraordinary event.

We used Cyril Ramaphosa and Roelf Meyer, leaders in South Africa who brought South Africa together in 1994 and the end of apartheid. It was a really fascinating use of the connections that we had, particularly O'Reilly, through his rugby, he played for the Lions in South Africa, and all those years later was able to use these connections to bring about a negotiation. One year after those meetings in South Africa, the Good Friday Agreement in Northern Ireland was signed. And I've spoken to many of the leaders since who've said it was that experience in South Africa, which was really a clinching element of that deal.

Kingsley Aikins

Why is networking now more important than ever?

Answer:
Oh yeah, well I would say it's more important than ever. It's a bit like asking a barber, do I need a haircut? Of course, you know, I'm just very passionate about why networking is so important. It's more important now than ever before, because we live in a totally interconnected, interdependent world. The world has changed quite dramatically. The

old sort of career structures we had, when people joined a company, worked, got promoted, we used to call it the Escalator Model of a career, that's all changed, that's all fundamentally different.

You need your networks to survive and thrive. This is something, which is, although it's always been with us, perhaps not at the same degree of momentum and trajectory as we have now. What people often don't realize is that as they progress through their career, the technical skills they needed in the first place to get into their jobs, become less important and relationships become more important. So now you've got all sorts of different elements out there.

Companies now want to hire and wire: they want to hire people and wire into their network. There's one very obvious reason why networking is more important than ever, more significant than ever, is that people who build strong and diverse networks live longer, are happier, earn more money, are more successful. So we live in a very diverse world, we live in a city here where 25 percent of the people in this city are not born in this country. We need to build diversity into our networks.

We need to build social capital as the resources available to you in your personal and business networks. We've got to use serendipity and luck to influence our lives. One connection can have an extraordinary effect on our lives. So, you know, I could go on about this at some length, but I just obviously, fundamentally, believe that this is going to be a key differentiating factor in this 21st century. People who've strong networks will be more successful.

Jeff Caselden

Tell me about a time where power was abused in a deal-closing context and led to sub-optimal outcomes for one or both sides.

Answer:
Yeah, I would certainly say that we abused our own power in this context, in some ways. We controlled the older product that this client we had was reliant upon and we were simply going to pull the plug on

it, unless they wanted to own it and support it for themselves, which they lacked both the technical expertise and resourcing to manage. So, migration to this new product was honestly their best viable alternative from the initial assessments done from each side. Though I can say that once things got tough, the other side kind of leveraged their own power in counter-productive ways, which actually eroded some of the traction we were managing to gain.

The leader we were dealing with on the other side of this deal had a real tendency to escalate issues to leadership unnecessarily and would get rather rude and somewhat hostile in his dealings with myself and our team. And, I mean, he certainly had reason to be unhappy, these engagements often did more damage, though, than they did to make things better.

https://expertdealcloser.com

Questions

1. What are the main types of corporate power?

Personal organizational power: Based on a person's position within the organization's hierarchy; Resources power; Shared history power; and Informational power.

2. Why are listening skills so important for deal-closing?

The best way to know what the other side wants is to ask them and then to actively listen to their response. By using active listening skills, you can pick up hints, clues and other signals from body language, movements, volume, and tone from which you ultimately may be able to assess the other side's positioning, likely flexibility and direction.

3. Why are networks and relationships so important to increase your information base and deal power?

The closer you get to knowing the intentions, desires and assumptions of the other side in a deal, the more likely you are to ultimately get what you want from the deal. Using networks and relationships is a very important additional way for deal-closers to gather the all-important information they need, which then enhances their knowledge and ultimately their power.

4. Give examples of useful ways to create, emphasize, or reinforce your deal-closing power?

SWOT; incentives; persuasion; alternative strategies; networks, contacts, and relationships; cultural awareness; using time-outs.

5. Why is a deal sheet useful?

A deal sheet is useful in terms of calibrating where the discussion is at, while also providing both sides with the ability to tweak and reframe their proposals as and when needed. Used the right way, deal sheets keep focus on the main issues at hand and confirm areas of agreement to date as well as outstanding action items.

They are especially useful where there are many complex, yet unrelated, issues at play. Also, a deal sheet is useful in calibrating whether you are falling short in any of your proposals.

https://expertdealcloser.com

CHAPTER 4

Players

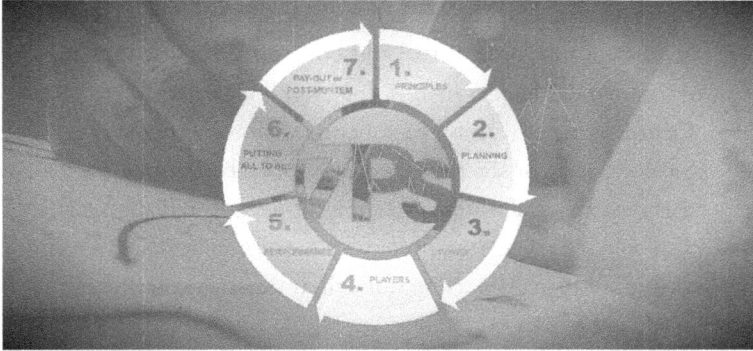

Great things in business are never done by one person. They're done by a team of people.

—IT entrepreneur, Steve Jobs

This chapter demonstrates how important the players involved in a deal are to the successful outcome of a deal.

Core Deal Team Roles

It is important to map out the key players on the other side as you are ultimately going to have to convince them all of your proposals. As part of the process of information gathering to bolster your deal-closing power base, you need to try and determine who is on the other side's deal team and each person's respective power, influence, and final say in the deal-closing process.

Generally speaking, while there are many potential categories and variations of deal team members and most roles often overlap, there are a few common core deal team roles:

- **Strategist**: This is the person who ultimately determines the deal strategy, the deal zone parameters, and often the deal finances. He or she may not be pivotal to the actual face-to-face deal discussions, but they will play an essential role in setting the deal direction;

- **Dealmaker**: This team member obviously leads the face-to-face deal discussions around the proposal, right through to the deal close;
- **Interpreter**: This team member usually focuses on information gathering and determining the other side's positioning and requirements. He or she is a diligent listener and watches and listens out for all verbal and non-verbal clues, and then recommends changes in deal direction if necessary;
- **Coordinator**: This team member needs to be as objective as possible, as he or she runs the deal process by keeping the discussion on track and managing the agenda and summaries. This role is particularly important in multi-issue deals, which are bound to get tense and difficult at times. A coordinator needs to be both firm and serene;
- **Implementer**: This team member is expert in successfully implementing the outcomes from a successful deal. I find this role is often lacking in a deal team and that the people making the deal will not always implement it operationally (which often leads to sub-optimal results).

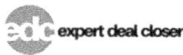

◐ expert deal closer   **Deal Team Roles**

Role	Responsibility	Our Team	Their Team
Strategist	• Determines deal strategy, deal zone parameters, & often the deal finances. • May not be pivotal to the actual face-to-face deal discussions, but will play an essential role in setting the deal direction.		
Dealmaker	• Leads the face-to-face deal discussions around the proposal, right through to the deal close.		
Interpreter	• Focuses on information gathering and determining the other side's positioning and requirements. • Is a diligent listener: ○ Watches and listens out for all verbal and nonverbal clues ○ Recommends changes in deal direction as necessary.		
Coordinator	• Runs the deal process by keeping the discussion on track and managing the agenda and summaries. • Crucial role in multi-issue deals. • A coordinator needs to be both firm and serene while remaining objective.		
Implementer	• Expert in successfully implementing the outcomes from a successful deal. • Often lacking in a deal team but crucial for optimal results.		

www.expertdealcloser.com

Sample Deal Team Roles Chart

Choose Your Deal Team Carefully

Regardless of your strategy and planning, the success of any deal is reliant upon the people involved.

There is real value, strength, and impetus to your deal-closing power in having a well-chosen, well-briefed, and well-run deal team. Of course, having the availability of an ideal deal team could be a luxury. Also, you are better off not having a team than having a badly chosen one.

Unless you are running a deal alone, which is rare from a corporate perspective, your choice of deal team is critically important as the shape of your team has a dramatic impact on your power (see Chapter 3). The right deal team members can enhance the knowledge, credibility, authority, and perception of your team. So, who to include, who to leave out, roles, and reporting methods are extremely important.

For example, there is nothing worse than the other side seeing your team at loggerheads and internally arguing. Disharmony is seen by the other side. Unfortunately, I have experienced the negative effects of the other side in a contract discussion seeing discord amongst stakeholders on my side of the deal. My overseas parent company was not as committed to local collaboration with the target company as its own local subsidiary, with which I was involved. This caused confusion and concern in the mind of the target company's senior management. And so, eventually, the deal did not transpire.

There is real value and strength and impetus to your deal-closing power in having a well-chosen, well-briefed, and well-run deal team.

Be Smart in Your Use of Experts

Always listen to experts. They'll tell you what can't be done, and why. Then do it.

—Science-fiction writer, Robert A. Heinlein

Simply put, lawyers, bankers, engineers, accountants, technicians, and other subject matter experts provide their expertise to the deal mix through their professional advice.

In my experience, the timing of their use is very much dependent on the specifics of each deal. One factor to consider is whether bringing in an expert assists or detracts from having sufficiently results orientated deal discussions—does it sharpen your deal position or conversely detract from this.

There is no definitive guidance as to when experts should be engaged in a deal journey. Cost is often a contributory factor though it can be false economy to bring them in too late just to save on costs. Also be aware that delaying the engagement of an expert may send a message to the other side that you are perhaps not sufficiently confident of your position to warrant the expense.

Speaking as a lawyer myself, your expert is only as good as his or her client's instructions (at least initially). So it is essential to brief your expert advisors as carefully and comprehensively as possible. As the old adage goes "garbage in, garbage out." And, of course, while your advisors can steer you, fundamentally they can only follow your instructions. It is up to you how much risk you are willing to take.

In structuring a recent business fund, our company was extremely careful to ensure that in our sub-manager's trust deed with our company's expertise was not only reflected accurately but also that our involvement as the expert in the field in question was accurately reflected at exactly the right times and in the right ways. The trust deed successfully encapsulated all this information because we went to great lengths to ensure that our advising lawyer knew what we were trying to achieve. Involving experts at the right time can enhance their effectiveness.

Work Out Who Is Who on the Other Side of the Table

You must never underestimate your opposition.
            —Former UK senior intelligence officer, John Scarlett

It is important to map out the key players on the other side of the deal table, as you are ultimately going to have to convince them all of your proposals. As part of the process of information-gathering to bolster your deal-closing power-base, you need to determine who is on the other side's deal team and each person's respective power, influence, and final say in the deal-closing process.

Assume at your peril that the other side's intentions are the same as your own. So, the more you understand the other side's motives, intentions, strengths, and weaknesses, the more you can use that to your advantage. Try to leverage a champion on the other side. Spending sufficient time to get to know, as much as you can, the people on the other side—their roles, motives, agendas, and so on—can only improve your chances of developing the all so important trust from the other side, which is like putting cash in the bank for the deal journey as a whole.

The Blocked Technology Deals

Again, back to the two blocked technology deals, it very quickly became clear to me that pass of the blockage was caused by a misunderstanding of who was on the other side's deal team.

Have you experienced this?

What did you do?

What did I do?

To move things along, I decided to determine very quickly who was on the other side's deal team and each person's respective power, perspective, and influence in the deal-closing process.

https://expertdealcloser.com

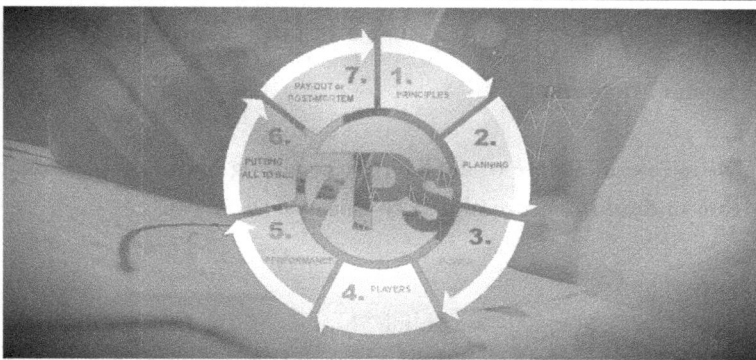

https://expertdealcloser.com

Summary

- Core deal team roles.
- Choose your deal team carefully.
- Be smart in your use of experts.
- Work out who is who on the other side of the table.

Executive Insights

Dermot Mannion

Tell me about a time where having the wrong player on your deal team undermined your ability to close a deal.

Answer:
There's no doubt that assembling the right team for a deal is very important. On the one hand, you want to have people along that will contribute constructively to the negotiations, but on the other hand though, in most organizations you have different constituencies of thought around the place, that needs to be represented in the team, as well.

So, the key thing really is, preparation getting the team into a conference room for preparatory sessions in advance of the meeting, so that you can create agreed positions across the group. And also, create a mechanism for identifying if there are any internal areas of disagreement in the negotiations, call a timeout, slip next door with your negotiating team, reestablish agreement on the relevant issue, and then go back in. The key thing to avoid is any sense that the other side can observe a sense of disagreement on your team. If you do that, it can have fatal consequences. So make sure you take your disagreements offline, outside the negotiating room.

Kingsley Aikins

Tell me about a time where leveraging experts was key in your ability to successfully close a deal.

Answer:
Well, certainly when I was working with the IDA, with the Trade Board, and was working with the Ireland Funds, bringing in outsiders who were experts and who really knew what was going on, was the added icing on the cake, if you like. I was just thinking of one particular example, when we had a very successful technology person from the West Coast, from Silicon Valley, who was passionate about music.

We arranged a dinner in the National Gallery in Ireland, we brought John O'Connor along, John O'Connor is a famed Irish musician. We actually had Seamus Heaney come and give support. We also had Gregory Peck, who was a film star from the United States come. And we used all these three people to create an extraordinary evening, very passionate evening. And toward the end of the evening, we asked this particular person would he be willing to fund John O'Connor to record all of Beethoven's Moonlight Sonatas. And of course, he did. It was a very significant contribution. It was using these outside influences to bring in an addition, if you like, to the overall impact to what we were trying to achieve.

Jeff Caselden

Tell me about a time where your awareness of the players on the other side of the table gave you a distinct advantage.

Answer:
Knowing the tendencies of this abrasive leader in this other team, I knew what failings he would be able to identify from my own team's work and that he would essentially use these as weapons in our next engagement. After a few of these run-ins, I adjusted my own style to take a much more self critical, transparent approach with him. In other words, I took the weapons he'd later try to use against us and I put them on the table first thing, full stop. So, without that card in his back pocket, he frankly didn't have the opportunity to lay into us and we were actually able to shift a lot of our conversations toward solutions to our mutual problems rather than these one-sided conversations about how we'd let him down. And it certainly meant that I had to dial back my own defensiveness, however, and my tendency to want to protect my own team.

https://expertdealcloser.com

Questions

1. What are the main deal team roles?

Strategist, dealmaker, interpreter, coordinator, and implementer.

2. Why is so important to choose the right deal team members?

The right deal team members can enhance the knowledge, credibility, authority, and perception of your team. So, who to include, who to leave out, roles, and reporting methods are extremely important.

3. Why is it so important to work out who is who on the other side of the deal table?

As part of the process of information-gathering to bolster your deal-closing power-base, you need to determine who is on the other side's deal team and each person's respective power, influence, and final say in the deal-closing process as you are ultimately going to have to convince them all of your proposals. The more you understand the other side's motives, intentions, strengths, and weaknesses, the more you can use that to your advantage.

https://expertdealcloser.com

CHAPTER 5

Performance

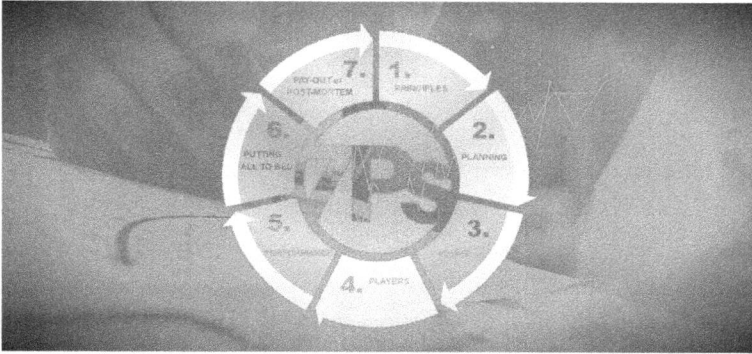

Under pressure, we perform as we've prepared.

—US pastor, Samuel Dueth

We have now arrived at a point on the deal journey where the deal has been planned, there is a strategy and an execution team in place. Now it is time for the deal encounter itself. This chapter demonstrates the fundamental importance of deal performance.

Structuring the Deal

Deals never structure themselves despite all the strategy, planning, and risk analysis in place. There are many issues that need to be resolved and catered for to ensure a deal performance transpires effectively. Matters such as parties, capital structure/providers/raising, financial and other due diligence, commercial, brand value impact, legal issues including agreements, taxation, and operational aspects all influence a deal process.

Timing is also always key. For example, in mergers and acquisitions deals, when potential targets become available, there can be irresistible pressure to buy. But in reality, owners of potential target companies know this and so often prepare their businesses for as inflated a sale price as possible. However, the optimal time to buy is usually determined when value creation can be optimized over a period of time—not when the seller wants it.

Risk mitigation is also critically important in maximizing a deal structure. The key in deal-closing is to maximize the upside opportunity of the deal in question while spreading downside risk of failure. Where a deal involves a merger, acquisition, corporate restructure, or similar strategic integration change, deal-closers need to have clear plans to facilitate the integration expeditiously and maximize economies of scale and efficiencies.

However, there is always the danger that such integrations can become protracted through complexities and resulting deal value and staff morale can decline. So accomplished deal-closers need to always have one eye on structuring the deal for optimal value realization, which can also mean proactively (a) investing in technology, systems, and processes; (b) bringing all key company stakeholders together throughout the process by embedding a deal value mindset within the organization. This involves asking whether targets are being met? If not, why and how can this be corrected?

Rehearse

While planning is critical, deal-closing is not just a theory exercise; practice does help to make perfect. So, in addition to planning all the strategic and tactical aspects of your deal journey, including team members and communication tactics, you should methodically rehearse how you will achieve your objectives and close the deal.

You have now identified and agreed on the primary and secondary issues to craft your final deal proposal. But you need to ensure you are giving yourself the best chance to seal the deal. Just as you would not appear on stage to deliver an important speech without first rehearsing it, you should not enter the closing phase of a deal without testing, substantiating and verifying your arguments, assumptions and general direction—and then doing it again (and again, if necessary!).

Rehearsing your close draws out any last-minute problems, issues, previously unidentified motivations, opinions, and anything else that could, at actual close, derail the deal.

I regularly rehearse how I will seal a deal that I am involved in. In one example, my consulting business was involved in leveraging State Government funding in Australia for a not-for-profit. We produced a contingency and opportunity analysis and then rehearsed all the possible issues that the State Government might need assurance over—and we prepared detailed answers to their questions. We were successful in leveraging the funds.

Be First to Propose

Being second is to be the first of the ones who lose.
—Motor racing legend, Ayrton Senna

Every deal involves three elements:

- An **offer**;
- A **counter-offer**; and
- A **close**.

Being first to make a proposal is very important in helping you to end up with the deal you want. This is primarily because, as humans, we tend to be heavily influenced by information that is offered to us first (this is sometimes referred to as "anchoring").

Do not wait for what the other side is prepared to give you. Instead, do your due diligence and then let the other side know what you are prepared to offer them. When you put an issue on the table first through your proposal, it places a line in the sand as the starting point of the discussion.

Always try to go first unless, for some reason, you have had little or no chance to do any due diligence—or somehow you are not, at that opening stage, aware of the true value in the deal and you therefore need to hedge your bets at this point.

If, for whatever reason, the other side goes first, reframe whilst thanking them for their suggestion—for example, "Thanks, but my proposal is … ." When the other side does makes an initial offer, use it as a means to be smart by eliciting information that is inconsistent with their first offer and then presenting it as a compelling alternative position.

As you know, there are three deal zone positions that you need to prepare for: likely, bottom-line, and opening. So, in making your proposal first, consider your likely outcome (what you realistically anticipate to achieve) to guide you in framing your opening position (the best possible position you can give away). Opening as high (or low, if you're selling) as reasonably possible provides you with the maximum amount of flexibility.

Open as Ambitiously as Possible

There is no formula for what you should open a deal with. Instead you must consider and balance many issues, such as relationships, where your company stands business-wise, who is in the deal room, and so on. In my experience, you will quickly know if you have not been ambitious enough—mainly from the speed at which the other side accepts your first proposal (of which, see more later).

Therefore, be sure you open as ambitiously as possible, though of course be mindful of cultural differences in the way you frame your opening. Also, try to avoid making an opening offer that could confuse or offend your counterpart. Unreasonable offers run the risk of provoking the other side to search for counter-arguments. The more you ask for, generally the more you can expect. Going first and as high as you can, you could end up achieving more than you might otherwise have done: you may make the other side believe they have won something by "bringing you down."

Be Smart in Framing Your Proposal

In making your proposal, be sure to carefully choose your words. Be as concise as possible and present your case in a logical, comprehensible, sequential way, for example by:

- **Introducing** your proposal;
- **Breaking down clearly** what you are saying by using facts and resisting the temptation to offer opinion. Do not be tempted to rush or skip primary issues. Be open to—and, in fact, encourage—interaction at this point;
- Trying to **get closure** by testing how the other side feels about each element of your proposal and ensuring you open the other side up as much as possible in terms of their thinking and direction. In presenting the first offer, make it as persuasive as possible by backing it up with a justification, and/or by adding novel, even more powerful information, such as confidential information or price variance; and
- **Repeating** all of the above until you are as confident as you can be that you can move on.

In making your proposal, you are effectively taking the other side on a deal journey with you. This is your chance to weave an image of the future that the other side will find it difficult to resist joining you in. When this is done well, it is replete with synchronicity, serenity, and not a little color. Here deal-closers with acting ambitions can shine.

A good deal requires momentum and you will struggle to get to a logical and satisfactory conclusion if you neglect this fact. It is up to you to patiently, but effectively, sweep the other side along with you in the steps required to reach a mutually satisfactory conclusion. If you experience blockages, awkward moments, or even deadlock in the process, then perhaps you are not maneuvering as adeptly as you could, or should, to ensure good momentum.

Pay careful attention at all times to the progress, words used, ongoing dynamics, and momentum of the deal. To help move the deal discussions forward it can, in certain circumstances, be helpful to be open about not only your needs and wants but also potential trade-offs. Of course, as part of your deal analysis, you should determine how safe it is to open up in this way.

Silence is powerful. I have experienced the other side opening up, and even increasing their proposal on occasion, rather than enduring the continuing wall of an awkward stony silence. I used this tactic to good effect when I was representing the European legal department of a U.S. technology company and charged with on-boarding a law firm to provide pan-European advice. Having received the firm's proposed engagement terms, I deliberately did not respond in the timeframe they had expected and allowed them to become aware that we were in discussion with an alternative service provider. Rather than wait for my counter-offer, the law firm volunteered a more favorable pricing structure, which we ultimately proceeded with.

In my experience, the following tactics can assist you in making and receiving deal proposals:

- Never show temper, defensiveness, irritability, confrontational style, or impatience;
- Ask questions and adapt your proposal and the general direction of the deal based upon the responses;
- Record all detail through note-taking and summarizing throughout;
- Do not interrupt or allow yourself to be interrupted.

A clever tactic to employ is "If you {do x], then I will [do y]." This demonstrates to the other side that you are prepared to help them, but they are going to have to work for that help. Offering a "give" but asking for a "take" in a deal can be a very powerful tool in framing proposals.

The Blocked Technology Deals

Over to the two blocked technology deals again, given the amount of time that had elapsed since the start of deal discussions before I was tasked to move the deals on, there was considerable confusion as to the status and progress of each side's historic proposals.

Have you experienced this?

What did you do?

What did I do?

To move things along, I decided to go back to basics and take the other side on a deal journey with me. I did this by carefully choosing my words and being as concise as possible in presenting the re-invigorated proposals, doing so in a logical, comprehensible, sequential way.

https://expertdealcloser.com

Good Communication Is Critical

The most important thing in communication is hearing what isn't said.

—Management consultant and educator, Peter Drucker

The "to and fro" and a successful deal is hinged upon both parties getting what they want from it. Good communication is critical for good deal-closing. Letting the other side know what you want and, at the same time, letting the other side be under the impression they can also get what they want in return, is essential. Listening to counter-proposals and being flexible during the entire process are also critically important.

A good deal-closer employs carefully selected words and uses smart gestures. He or she also actively listens to the words used by the other side, while being very alert to their subtle signs, gestures, and other clues. But, be aware that, even with language itself (let alone non-verbal communication), there are vast differences between cultures that give different meanings to certain words such as "reasonable" or "progress."

Types of Communication

Oxford Dictionaries—Language Matters defines communication as *The imparting or exchanging of information by speaking, writing, or using some other medium.*

From this definition you can see that there are two major types of communication:

Verbal communication: this includes not only speech, but also forms of writing/uses of symbols and sign language. In turn, there are two major types of verbal communication:

(a) *Conscious verbal communication*—this occurs where we are aware of the words and symbols we are using. It is the most common type of verbal communication. The most accomplished deal-closers are adept as using clear and measured communication, being aware of what they need to say, how and when to say it. They are also aware of what the other side hears, its impact and potential responses and when to ask questions, actively listen, summarize the status of the interaction, and clarify understandings to minimize misunderstandings.

(b) *Unconscious verbal communication*—this occurs where we are not fully aware of what we are actually saying. We need to pick up on the clues of any unconscious verbal communication from the other side. For example, look out for repeated use of certain words such as "*yes*" or saying "*right*" to help you understand what might be of most importance to the other side and areas for opening opportunity.

Non-verbal communication: this includes engagement other than by words or symbols, such as through physical gestures and other body language including eye contact and posture.

While useful, this form of communication is not as reliable to interpret as verbal communication and you need to be very careful not to frame your deal strategy purely on this. Body language varies with gender, cultural, and generational differences. For example, we are all aware of the stereotypes of German efficiency, Latino passion, and Asian collectivity. But stereotypes are easily adapted and masked so while an awareness of them is important, just as important is the need for constant calibration and situational assessment.

Finally, there are those elements of body language, which are termed micro-expressions, such as pupil dilation, blushing, muscle spasms, and so on. While often meaningful, these reflexive expressions are probably on the whole left to experts to interpret. That said, taken as a whole, they can add to the overall tapestry of communication.

Human Behavior Trumps Facts

I have rarely been in a deal meeting without seeing human emotions and behaviors rise to the surface. Deal-closing is as much—if not more—about human behavior as it is about the facts, processes, and systems you use or engage in during a deal.

Whether we want to own up to it or not, we are both consciously and subconsciously influenced by what we see and hear in the other person; their appearance, race, age, gender, and so on. All these subconscious biases can, for better or for worse, impact upon how we see the other side and how we behave within the deal.

Human behavior can be challenging at times (aggressive, bullying, or threatening, for example). No matter how well prepared you are, unhelpful behaviors can throw you off track in the heat of the moment. Worse still, I have experienced such behavior being used in an attempt to derail me and/or increase the perception of the other side's power. Of course, you can attempt to minimize these behaviors by, for example, ignoring them, pre-empting them (by way of advanced planning) or calling them out for what they are.

You also cannot always anticipate unpredictability within the opposing team. For example, even though you think you may be making progress with the other side's dealmaker or head negotiator, he or she may struggle to sell your proposal to his or her team or wider corporate stakeholders. This may result in a surprising change in emphasis or direction, or even new demands.

But, if you really concentrate on the other side's behavior, you significantly increase your chances of deal-closing success. Most behavior is observable and therefore being able to join the strands between observable behavior, business needs, and personal wants is a critical skill for expert deal-closing. It is important that you concentrate as fully as you can on how you come across, what you are saying, what you are not saying and your body language. Try using firm language and a deeper voice and look comfortable, composed, and authoritative, whilst being conscious of (and if necessary, addressing) your own movements.

Of course, a deal team needs to ensure that it has the approval of its own organization, which can, particularly in large, multi-layered and siloed organizations, be difficult. Letting the other side know of your organizational mandate is also important from a power perception perspective.

Use Deadlines as a Focusing Tactic

It is wise when you are leading the discussion to set time expectations. Nothing focuses the mind better than a deadline. In addition, deadlines can force people (including you) to agree to things that they normally would not, so deadlines can be a double-edged sword. Nonetheless, time is a key factor in ensuring sufficient preparation and planning for the deal. Be diligent in your use of time—to avoid being pressured.

That said, there is a fine line between managing the course of the deal on the one hand and being seen to want to rush things for your own good. You need to be tactful and situation-aware when setting deadlines.

Dermot Mannion has a distinguished career in aviation and technology, including as former CEO of Aer Lingus, Deputy Chairman of Royal Brunei Airline and President Group Support Services at Emirates. Dermot carries significant experience in the area of deal execution.

Dermot is a strong believer in the critical importance of setting and striving to meet realistic deadlines in negotiations. In his view, once the timetable is in place it is then all about creating and maintaining momentum to ensure the deadlines are achieved. At the same time, Dermot emphasizes that skilled negotiators do need to "keep an eye on" matters away from the negotiating table to ensure all stakeholders are kept regularly appraised of developments. "No one in authority likes to get nasty surprises in the concluding stages of a negotiation" he points out.

This highlights the critical need to ensure that the internal corporate deal approval process is set up and ready to respond when the final transaction documents come to hand. "Executive management committees and Boards of Directors will have their own corporate governance procedures to follow. This takes time and such requirements need to be built into the timeline" says Mr. Mannion.

Incentives Always Appeal

Call it what you will, incentives are what get people to work harder.
—Former Soviet President, Nikita Khrushchev

Deal-closing is not an objective, emotionless activity, operating separate from the vagaries of human sentiment, emotion, wants, and needs. That's why incentives work.

To successfully use incentives to reel in a deal, again you need to know what is important to the other side. To be attractive, the incentive must obviously address the other party's needs and wants. Asking questions and truly hearing the answers, through active rather than passive listening, is the only way to find out.

But the best way to get what you want in a deal is by offering the other party what satisfies their needs through the value transaction. In my experience, the more value-based incentives you can find to entice the other party, the more interest they are likely have in doing the deal with you. For example, in order to leverage a joint venture agreement in the resources industry in Australia, I used incentives in the form of a last-minute preferential shareholding offer in the new venture to seal the deal. This was what persuaded the other, larger company, to proceed; without the incentive, the deal might not have gone ahead.

It's Not Over Until It's Over

But I don't want to leave until I see the breakthrough.
—Actor and screenwriter, Stephen Lewis

Sometimes the deal discussions will grind to a halt for a variety of reasons, intentional or unintentional. This is why getting your planning and preparation for power as right as possible is so important in terms of anticipating as many eventualities as possible. When a deal grinds to a halt, the flow-on implications can be dangerous, including lost or irretrievable time, financial loss, structural impacts, or damaged egos.

Deals can become intentionally blocked, because the other side:

- Feels their bottom line has been transgressed;
- Perceives lack of value or too high a cost;
- Is overwhelmed by ego, face, or obstinacy, or their game plan is to play hardball with litigation and sue out of tactic or indeed principle;
- After all, prefers the status quo;
- Considers that the business or corporate environment has changed.

Whatever the case, you must efficiently determine what is causing the blockage and deal with it quickly and comprehensively. When blockages occur, I find it helpful to ask clarifying questions, such as:

- "Under what circumstances would you be willing to x;"
- "Is there anything I can do to help move this on;"
- "Are there any conditions that, if satisfied, would allow you to move on."

I have seen occasions when neither side is willing to move ground from their likely outcome. However, usually a pathway through is possible, but you will need to summon all your skills to save and/or move the deal forward by cleverly, flexibly, and swiftly presenting proposals and solutions to unblock the stalemate. Don't necessarily expect to get a quick breakthrough but, if you are patient and tactful, you give yourself the best possible chance to eventually find a proposal that will sufficiently resonate with the other side to unblock the impasse.

In some cases, it may be wiser to engage a trusted third party, such as a mediator. Both parties then disclose their respective bottom lines to him or her, with a view to a deal being reached within a zone of possible agreement. Of course, this is not always possible and a walk-away ultimately might be necessary.

Getting a Deal Back on Track

If a deal derails, you can try to get the discussions back on track by changing your deal team, making a new proposal or reframing your existing proposal. Other tactics include altering your deal zone parameters, calling a "cooling off" time-out or escalating the matter to your boss. Be careful before you escalate to your boss as this may suggest to the other side that you perhaps do not have the degree of authority that your originally represented, thereby potentially weakening your bargaining position. It may be better, optics wise, to keep your boss behind the scenes but updated unless or until there is a deadlock requiring a change of input.

If things are going wrong (and believe me they do), it is far preferable to adjourn a deal meeting than to carry on with a deal you know will fail. I often find that the very act of adjournment can itself refocus thinking and provide the parties with an opportunity to get back on track by recalibrating both sides' assumptions, expectations, and desired outcomes.

Don't Walk Away Too Early

Don't forget that just because the deal is not proceeding does not mean you have not done everything possible to finalize it. The other side's reasons may not be related to your deal-closing abilities. For example, their hands may be tied by circumstances in their own company or even from a macro-economic perspective.

As a very last resort, consider walking away from the deal only if it becomes clear that you are just not going to get anywhere. But you need to be very sure that a deal is not going to happen—in my experience, people throw in the towel too early, only to regret it later.

I made this mistake myself in some choppy negotiations involving a Chinese company. Through a series of misunderstandings, miscommunications, and no doubt cultural barriers, I walked away from a deal that I believed would never happen. With hindsight, I could have been a little more patient and tactful, but even the best deal-closers don't always get it right. However, an upside is that I am now better able to distinguish between when I need to walk away and when I am allowing my emotions to overrule common-sense.

That said, there are for me some lines that I will simply not cross: being asked to compromise my ethics or to deal below my bottom line. In either case, I always walk away. My advice to you is to do the same.

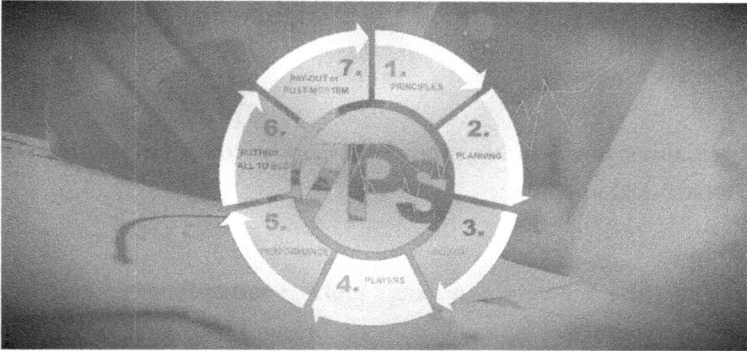

https://expertdealcloser.com

Summary

- Structuring the deal.
- Rehearse.
- Be first to propose.
- Open as ambitiously as possible.
- Be smart in framing your proposal.
- Good communication is critical.
- Human behavior trumps facts.
- Use deadlines as a focusing tactic.
- Incentives always appeal.
- It's not over until it's over.
- Getting a deal back on track.
- Don't walk away too early.

Executive Insights

Dermot Mannion

Talk about how you have seen behaviors or communication styles impact deal outcomes.

Answer:
For me, the key communication tool for successful negotiations is injecting humor at the right moment. I mean I have been in negotiating rooms where the tension was palpable, where you really are down to the last three or four high-tension issues. Inject a little humor into the conversation. Suddenly the atmosphere lightens on both sides of the table and you are creating an atmosphere in which the deal can get done. So, using humor at the right time in the right place is a key benefit.

Jeff Caselden

Talk about how you have seen behaviors or communication styles impact deal outcomes.

Answer:
Yes, the one leader I've described through much of this story ended up hiring another senior manager who reported directly to him and decided that seeing this project through would be one of his first tasks in the new team. I took this as an opportunity to really start afresh from a clean slate with this individual who had been delegated the project.

As a consequence, we built a much more open and honest relationship from the get go. I still had to approach the situation quite similarly knowing that the old boss was still in the way there and just a layer away and that he was highly interested in overseeing the outcome that we were looking for here. However, without that former leader as my direct contact, the levels of animosity between our teams and our collective ability to move forward on the project really began to see strong improvements.

https://expertdealcloser.com

Questions

1. **Why is it so important to make try and make the first proposal?**

   Being first to make a proposal is very important in helping you to end up with the deal you want. This is primarily because, as humans, we tend to be heavily influenced by information that is offered to us first (this is sometimes referred to as "anchoring").

   Do not wait for what the other side is prepared to give you. Instead, do your due diligence and then let the other side know what you are prepared to offer them. When you put an issue on the table first through your proposal, it places a line in the sand as the starting point of the discussion.

2. **How do you know if you have opened your deal discussions sufficiently ambitiously?**

   You will quickly know if you have not been ambitious enough—mainly from the speed at which the other side accepts your first proposal.

   Be sure you open as ambitiously as possible, though of course be mindful of cultural differences in the way you frame your opening. The more you ask for, generally the more you can expect.

3. **What tactics can be used in making and receiving deal proposals?**

   Never show temper, defensiveness, irritability, confrontational style, or impatience.

   Ask questions and adapt your proposal and the general direction of the deal based upon the responses. Record all detail through note taking and summarizing throughout. Do not interrupt or allow yourself to be interrupted. A clever tactic to employ is "If you {do x}, then I will [do y]." This demonstrates to the other side that you are prepared to help them, but they are going to have to work for that help.

4. How do you maximize use of incentives in deal-closing

To be attractive, an incentive must obviously address the other party's needs and wants. Asking questions and truly hearing the answers, through active rather than passive listening, is the only way to find out.

The best way to get what you want in a deal is by offering the other party what satisfies their needs through the value transaction. The more value-based incentives you can find to entice the other party, the more interest they are likely have in doing the deal with you.

5. Give some examples of when a deal might become intentionally blocked.

Deals can become intentionally blocked, because the other side: feels their bottom line has been transgressed; perceives lack of value or too high a cost; is overwhelmed by ego, face, or obstinacy, or their game plan is to play hardball with litigation and sue out of tactic or indeed principle; after all, prefers the status quo; considers that the business or corporate environment has changed.

https://expertdealcloser.com

CHAPTER 6

Putting It All to Bed

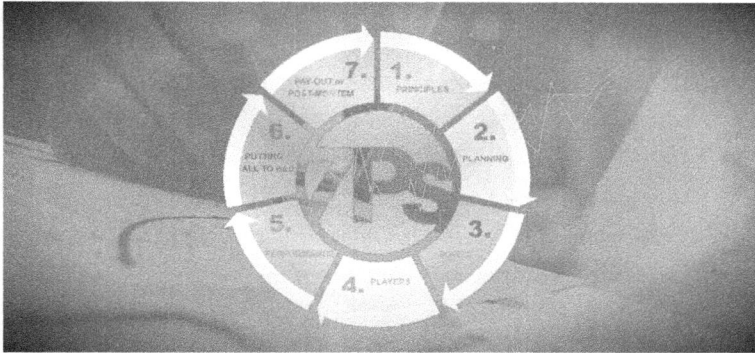

Everything has to come to an end, sometime.
—L. Frank Baum, author of *The Wizard of Oz*

You have now arrived at the all-important finale, having expended a huge amount of time and energy to get to this point. You have strategized, planned, developed and used relationships and networks, built a team, made and received proposals, reconsidered and thrown in a fair amount of psychology, patience, wisdom, and fortitude to boot. The last thing you want to do is let yourself down now. So this chapter looks at last-minute checks and other tactics to use when you reach the deal close.

Check That Nothing Has Been Left Off the Table

At this stage, just as a deal is about to close, I use a brief checklist of questions to make sure there is nothing still to be discussed. Over the course of my career, operating at senior management levels internationally, I have found this checklist invaluable before the parties step into the actual deal closure.

Example Checklist for a Joint Venture

A brief checklist of questions in order to find out whether there is anything still to be discussed.

- Have we left anything out of the Joint Venture deal discussions to date?
- Is there anything that was not raised in the discussions that we should now raise that will impact upon the Joint Venture?
- Are we proceeding with an Incorporated Joint Venture? If not, are we proceeding with an Unincorporated Joint Venture?
- Are the ownership stakes in the Joint Venture equal? If not, what are they?
- Is the profit split in the Joint Venture equal? If not, what is it?
- Are capital contributions required for the Joint Venture? If so, what are they?
- Are one or both parties contributing intellectual property to the Joint Venture? If so, list it.
- Are one or both parties contributing property or equipment to the Joint Venture? If so, list it.
- Are one or both parties contributing contracts to the Joint Venture? If so, list them.
- Will the Joint Venture have a Management Committee? If so, who will it comprise?
- Will the Joint Venture expire after a fixed period of time? If so, what will that period be?
- Is there anything else that we should add to these Joint Venture discussions?
- Are we both happy to now close these Joint Venture discussions?

I have learnt to use closed questions where possible, so that simple "Yes" or "No" answers can be given. For example, a "No" answer to "Have we left anything out of the deal discussions to date?" is an unambiguous agreement to move forward to conclude the deal, while a "Yes" to the same question means there's still work to be done. The converse applies to "Are you now in a position to close?" If you can get the opposing deal-closer or chief negotiator to confirm that all is on track for a successful deal, then you are well set up to seal the deal.

Clarify Mutual Understanding

Once you have finished the checklist questions, pay attention to your own instincts. Are you happy with where things are heading? Are all the members of your team happy?

Dermot Mannion makes the point that "the key to the successful conclusion of any negotiation is to keep onside all your internal constituencies (represented both inside and outside the deal room)." According to Mr. Mannion "this is achieved by letting all vested interests have their say and then arrive at a collective decision on the way forward." If internal areas of disagreement emerge, then take "a time out to regroup and resolve." Mr. Mannion also emphasizes the importance of having on the deal team "people who know their way around the organization and you are capable of resolving any issues which may arise at a departmental level promptly."

Can you sense any dissent among them? In my experience, there is nothing more toxic than a disaffected member of the opposing side whispering negatives behind the scenes.

Check for mutual understanding on all the key points of the deal. This is where your deal summary (see Chapter 3) is invaluable. Surprising as it may seem, I have seen deals derail at this point when the parties realize that unrecognized differences, no matter how subtle, exist in each other's understanding of the deal. So, you must try to verify, before you move to close the deal, that you are both about to sign the same deal and that no further adjustments or recalibrations are necessary.

I have found this clarification step particularly important when working with different cultures or languages. For example, in assisting the brokering of an Australian pharmacy chain supply deal into the Chinese market, I found it absolutely vital to keep summarizing each side's position, summarizing the deal at every stage, and particularly at this pre-close stage. Again, where humans are involved, underestimate at your peril the possibility of misunderstanding.

The Deal Is Not Over When You Shake Hands

As we saw in Chapter 5, it is not over until it is over. Even though you have rehearsed the close and have established the ostensible confirmation of the opposing team, you still need to "cross some Ts" and "dot some Is" in sealing the deal. A lot of people mistakenly think that the deal is over when you shake hands. That is not the case. In my experience, one of the most arduous—and yet important—parts of a deal is summarizing the deal in writing to protect both parties' interests post-agreement.

Summarize the deal at this point and compare where you have landed with the deal against your likely outcome (hopefully, rather than your bottom line) of your deal zone. If you have fallen short, you have one last chance now to try adjusting the deal parameters, though I have rarely seen this happen at this late stage. If you are successful in reframing the discussion and you achieve positive movement in the deal, then ensure that the other side explicitly agrees that this is their new understanding so as to minimize the possibility of any later conflict.

Then, whatever you have managed to achieve through skilled deal-closing, I strongly encourage you to get the deal memorialized in writing via a memorandum of understanding, letter of intent term sheet, heads of agreement, or some other (preferably, legally-binding) instrument. This should be done straight away before there is any room for second thoughts, or before circumstances change. Sign while the excitement is high and before second-guessing and doubt kicks in.

Even then, I strongly recommend that you future-proof your agreement by inserting performance KPIs, trigger points, service level agreements and regular, formal and informal review points to give yourself an opportunity to unravel the deal (or parts of it) further down the track for any non-delivery, poor performance or other similar failures by the other side. But don't overdo this—there's a fine balance here.

This is not the glamorous end of the deal-closing journey, but I have seen last minute problems arise when this part of the journey is rushed. In fact, as a former litigator, I know from first-hand experience that lack of attention to memorializing the deal causes a large number of commercial disputes. This is where it often pays to bring in an expert advisor, usually a lawyer.

Try—at all costs—not to allow the other side to write up the deal memorandum. It is better if you (or your advisors) draft the deal memorandum rather than risk needing to revise a document drafted by the other side's advisors.

Finally, instead of getting bogged down in dealing with every minor detail, you are better advised to try and pull all points into a more holistic, global conclusion. Make sure the terms of the agreement are concise, clear and as unequivocal as possible. Ensure individuals from both sides are explicitly involved in approving and signing off the final contract. Record in a note that they were present so as to help avoid any future dispute about misguided intention.

Dermot Mannion, has clear views about closing out final issues in a deal discussion:

- Avoid getting bogged down on tricky negotiation points;
- Always focus on the big picture;
- Leave the subject matter experts to resolve complex indemnity provisions;
- Use an iterative process to seek to close out issues "one by one;"
- Each time you "sweep" the document you get closer and closer to "sign off;"
- This serves to build trust and confidence in achieving a positive final outcome; and
- Most importantly, making step by step progress builds momentum.

He also emphasizes the importance of "holding everyone's feet to the fire until the final wording is agreed":

- Nothing is agreed until everything is agreed;
- "In principle" agreement is not usually conclusive;
- Keep all the deal team in the room until the deal wording is finalized;
- Once the deal team disperses cracks can arise;

- New and real areas of disagreement often arise in resolving the legal wording; and
- Constant vigilance is required until the deal is fully executed.

Governance and Risk

Good deal-closers and deal-making organizations have in place solid deal governance and risk systems and processes for all stages of deal processes, due diligence procedures and supporting deal frameworks, systems and culture. Such processes could include setting clear activities for each stages of the deal, allowing for more informed decisions about whether or not the deal in question should continue and how.

As Dermot Mannion points out: "deal makers move on and it is critically important to ensure that corporate knowledge of transactions is retained in the business." Critically this is achieved by:

- Maintaining a central repository of all corporate agreements;
- Ensuring the transaction file contains a concise summary of the transaction;
- Creating a corporate diary of important contractual milestone dates;
- Ensuring the important deadline dates are not missed; and
- Using the corporate risk register to record and monitor transaction risks.

The Blocked Technology Deals

Once again, back to the two blocked technology deals. While I had reached the stage of closing in on mutually satisfactory deals, I noticed that there had not hitherto been great deal of attention spent on future-proofing any possible deals reached.

Have you experienced this?

What did you do?

What did I do?

To memorialize things, I carefully inserted performance KPIs and both formal and informal review points in the deals to cover as many non-delivery, non-performance eventualities as possible.

https://expertdealcloser.com

Agree on the Implementation Plan Prior to Execution

You have done it. Your final proposal has been accepted and the deal has been summarized and accepted. However, despite the natural elation of both parties, this is yet another point in the deal prior to contract signing where I have seen deals fall away or unravel.

You need to agree on the deal implementation plan or the mechanisms for actually implementing the deal. It is really important to do so at this point, as you do not want to set unachievable activity and implementation goals that may result in dispute at a later date.

You also need to be mindful of data storage, record-keeping, management, privacy issues.

Prepare for Divorce: Just in Case

Finally, I tell all my clients to ensure that they incorporate a mediation or arbitration clause in their deal contract—just in case. It is always better to be prepared for the "divorce," in case it arrives. A simple, uncomplicated, well-drafted dispute resolution clause can—and, in my experience, often does—stave off the potential distraction of misunderstanding and ongoing debate.

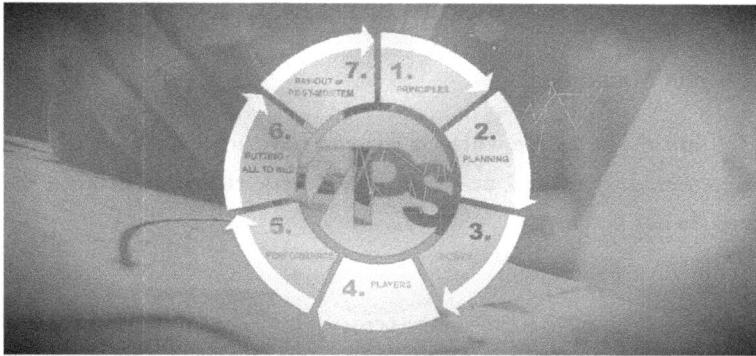

https://expertdealcloser.com

Summary

- Check that nothing has been left off the table.
- Clarify mutual understanding.
- The deal is not over when you shake hands.
- Governance and risk.
- Agree on the implementation plan prior to execution.
- Prepare for divorce—just in case.

Executive Insights

Dermot Mannion

Tell me about a time where it felt you have achieved your desired outcome only to find an unaddressed issue risked or delayed the conclusion.

Answer:

Well, what tends to happen here is that it is important in negotiations that you not just agree issues in principle with the other side, but you actually get the documentation done, as well. So in other words, in my view, no issue is agreed until not only is it agreed in principle but you actually get the words down into the document. If you do that, section-by-section as you move through the document, you will reduce significantly the risk of any unexpected issues coming up at the end.

Jeff Caselden

Discuss how you have seen performance metrics or KPIs become critical to helping secure a deal?

Answer:

Sure, as we went down the road of recovering this relationship and delivering the product solution we set out to achieve for this customer, we obviously hit a number of hurdles and we had lost significant trust along the way. And at several junctures we had made commitments, which we frankly just ended up not being able to deliver. And it was no shock to think that our customer might not believe further commitments that we made. But one of the ways in which I was able to get them onboard with our final solution was to build in strong performance targets and agreements. These were beyond dates and deadlines, these were hard KPIs, which put our development and our operations teams' money where our mouth was. So, we ended up getting agreement and backing from our own leadership to stand behind what we were now asserting, and we wouldn't be able to skirt issues as we previously had.

https://expertdealcloser.com

Questions

1. **What are some ways you can future proof your deal agreement?**

   You can insert performance KPIs, trigger points, service level agreements and regular, formal and informal review points to give yourself an opportunity to unravel the deal (or parts of it) further down the track for any non-delivery, poor performance or other similar failures by the other side. But don't overdo this—there's a fine balance here.

2. **Even though the deal has been summarized and accepted what should you still do besides future-proofing your deal?**

   You need to agree on the deal implementation plan or the mechanisms for actually implementing the deal. It is really important to do so at this point, as you do not want to set unachievable activity and implementation goals that may result in dispute at a later date.

https://expertdealcloser.com

CHAPTER 7

Pay-Out or Post-Mortem

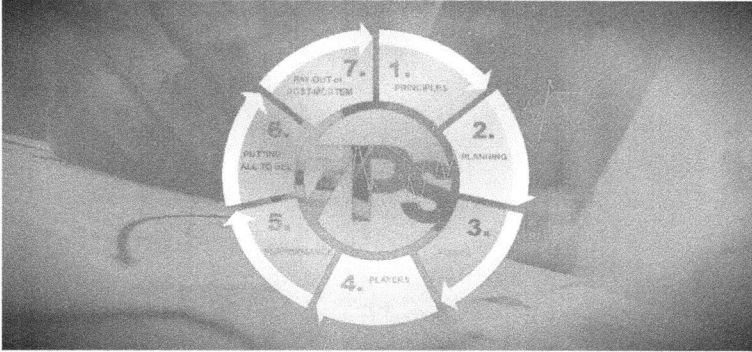

A rejection is nothing more than a necessary step in the pursuit of success.

—Businessman, Bo Bennett

Job done—this is when you can sit back and take credit for a successful deal execution. But, sometimes, closing a deal is not always possible and you need to learn not to take such occasions to heart. Nonetheless, every deal—successful or otherwise—contains within it learnings for the future. As I said at the start of this book, successful deal-closing is at least in part a matter of practice.

Measure Every Deal Success-Wise

From a corporate growth perspective, you should ideally have systems in place to measure success in terms of striking the deal—on every deal from a process, pace, and direction perspective. These systems should monitor all aspects of the deal performance, outcomes, and indeed, even in the learnings you take from a failed deal. Executing a successful deal is rarely a simple or easy undertaking. Deals usually swing and sway from their original strategic, financial, or operational imperatives and can look substantially different at the end of the process.

At the end of a deal, when perhaps you least feel like it, you really should schedule some time to methodically review the key areas of the deal journey, the outcomes, learnings, and areas for improvement for future deals and to note newly introduced tactics that worked well and could be used again in future.

As part of your deal review process, you should ideally identify items that went well and those did not so as to maximize deal chances next time around. Even better, if you can afford an independent benchmarking analysis, then it might be worthwhile to consider this. The sort of matters that could be examined include: (a) how the deal process added value to the general organizational value; (b) how learnings from the deal process were captured in the organizational knowledge management structures; (c) the degree to which the organization and its stakeholders may have aligned or otherwise during the deal process; and (d) the balance between short term gains and longer term organizational value creation.

Don't Be Hard on Yourself

Despite your best efforts in putting a good deal on the table, the vagaries of deal-closing (as referenced throughout this book) mean that things can—and often do—go wrong. Not all deal discussions will result in a successful deal. Sometimes deadlock or dispute will arise (see Chapter 5 for advice on getting a deal back on track).

Be aware that a "No" from the other side does not always mean the deal is at an end. Too often parties walk away at this point, but many times in deal discussions I have heard "No" and yet I have seen a way forward. A good deal-closer will use "No" as a cue to reframe and try a new tactic.

Be aware too that not consummating a deal does not always mean failure. It might even be the right outcome—perhaps there wasn't really a deal there. I have seen this occur, for example, because despite the strategic appeal the numbers just did not work out or because the proposed arrangement was not in the longer-term business interests of one or both parties.

An example of this occurred during the year I spent working on a significant, and potentially lucrative, deal for a resources company. The strategy made sense, the numbers stacked up and the deal would have brought good immediate returns. However, macro-economic circumstances changed during the year, including a significant drop in the value of the commodity in question, so ultimately the deal could not—and did not—proceed. Far from regarding the unsuccessful deal as a failure, we concluded that perhaps we had had a lucky escape!

Instead of failing or collapsing, a deal might just be drifting too far to one side to continue in its current guise. Here, it might be possible to suggest a time out and a revised negotiation process, but this will of course require solid relationship foundations to date and common grounds for value. Alternatively, depending upon how things are going, you could make alternative offers in relation to key components of the deal discussion, such as price, contract duration, and other key terms.

Beware also the magic "Yes" that comes too easily. If you have received a "Yes" response to your proposal too quickly, it might actually mean that you have misinterpreted the deal landscape and therefore have opened too easily. Deal-closing is about getting to the right deal through a process, not about capitulating early to get the deal done.

The Blocked Technology Deals

For the final time, back to the two blocked technology deals, on a few occasions, I reached seemingly intractable impasses with the other side.

Have you experienced this?

What did you do?

What did I do?

To move things along, rather than simply raise the white flags, I used "No" as a cue to reframe and try a new tactic.

And the outcome—I'm pleased to say that, following a two-year impasse, I managed to unblock both deals worth many hundreds of millions of dollars. Deal done.

https://expertdealcloser.com

Conduct a Formal Post-Mortem on Your Deal Journey

Win or lose, ensure you capture your learnings to use in the next deal by doing a formal post-mortem of your whole deal journey.

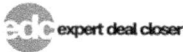

edc expert deal closer Deal Performance Post-mortem

	Outcomes	Learnings	Areas for Improvement	Newly Introduced & Successful Tactics (for future reference)
Principles				
Planning				
Preparing for Power				
Players				
Performance				
Putting it All to Bed				
Pay-out or Post-mortem				

www.expertdealclosers.com

Sample Deal Post-Mortem Chart

In conducting your post-mortem analysis be sure to be as comprehensive as possible in analyzing all financial, commercial, operational, and any post-deal integration matters. Of course, systems must be in place to ensure that the information you use is accurate and up-to-date, while allowing for measurement of ongoing continuous improvement. Your post-mortem should, of course, have systems to measure success to include factors such as $ results, cost efficiencies and savings, stakeholder engagement and satisfaction, operational efficiencies, innovation, and so on.

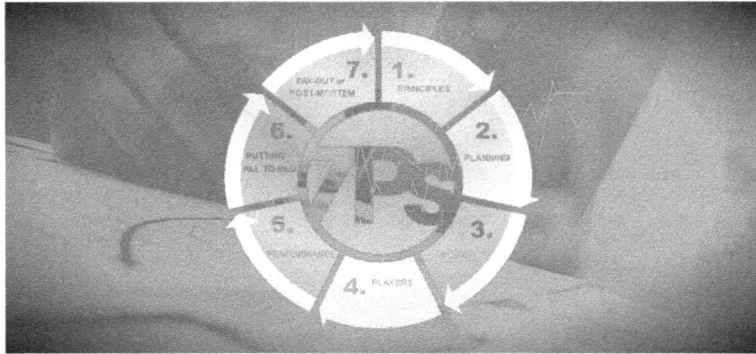

https://expertdealcloser.com

Summary

- Measure every deal success-wise.
- Don't be hard on yourself.
- Conduct a formal post-mortem on your deal journey.

Executive Insights

Dermot Mannion

Tell me about one of your biggest learnings that you took away from hindsight in your deal-closing experience.

Answer:
For me, it is all about momentum. Keep the negotiations going. You know, when you start going through the documentation, do not get bogged down on the first point of disagreement. Simply note it and move on. Sweep through the document, get to the end. What you will probably find is that, first time round there will be thirty areas of disagreement, the second time you sweep the document, you could be down to twenty, and ten. We call this the process of successive approximation. Eventually, you will get to the end and you'll be down to just two or three issues and you're creating a much better climate in which to resolve those and get the deal done.

Kingsley Aikins

How have post-mortem exercises revealed important new improvements in how you conducted future deal-closing exercises?

Answer:
Well, I think I mentioned earlier about how there were four phases and we divided all four phases to doing our business, which were research, cultivation, solicitation and the ask, and then the final piece-stewardship, which is kind of after the deal has happened. We found that was a really important part because we sensed every deal was just a down payment on the next deal. But, you know, all the research shows that the reason why people give up doing business with another organization is because they detect a sense of indifference toward them. In other words, we take the deal for granted. In fact, we just do not make enough fuss about them in many ways.

So we had a whole stewardship program where we thanked people five different ways, we were consistently using other people to thank them, we were always asking and trying to find out why people were doing business with us. Certainly, we wanted to see would they refer us to other people. All those things improved the information bank of knowledge we had about why the deal was successful, what are the elements we learned from it, and what can we change going forward for future deals.

Jeff Caselden

Tell me about one of your biggest learnings that you took away from hindsight in your deal-closing experience.

Answer:

Yes, absolutely, I think the biggest one for me in this case was to know exactly what you are selling and the service you are providing, inside and out. In this scenario, as I mentioned, I came in a bit later to the game as an "account manager" for this client, and well after the initial negotiations and plans had been set out. The more time I spent in this situation, the more apparent and clear it became to me that in many ways, we had sort of advertised a Mercedes but sold the client a Yugo. We simply could not deliver on the expectations we set, and without a really clear sense of what our client needed and valued, we created a scenario for ourselves where we really were not going to come out as winners. At least not without some serious pain along the way.

https://expertdealcloser.com

Questions

1. **What should your systems to measure the success of the deal struck monitor?**

   These systems should monitor all aspects of the deal performance, outcomes and, indeed, even in the learnings you take from a failed deal.

2. **Can a failed deal ever be a good result?**

   "No" from the other side does not always mean the deal is at an end. Too often parties walk away at this point, but many times in deal discussions we have heard "No" and yet we have seen a way forward. A good deal-closer will use "No" as a cue to reframe and try a new tactic.

   Be aware too that not consummating a deal does not always mean failure. It might even be the right outcome—perhaps there wasn't really a deal there.

https://expertdealcloser.com

CHAPTER 8

Conclusion

If you need to make deals—*business agreements or arrangements* for corporate growth—you need to know how to play the "deal-game." I have summarized the key prerequisites for deal-making success from this book as follows.

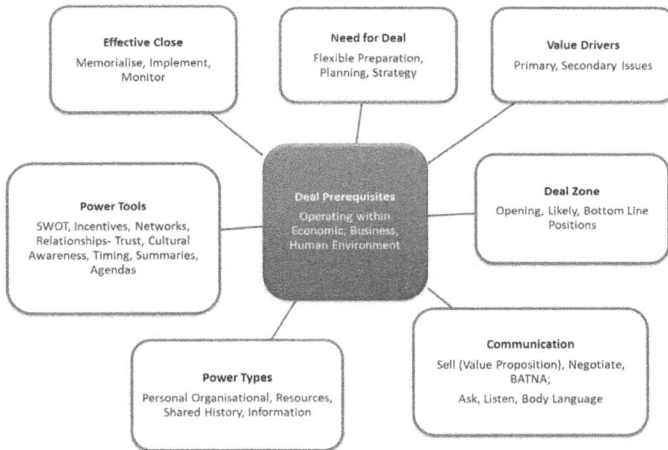

In turn, to summarize key ingredients for better individual deal-closing:

- Understand and support your bargaining power—emotional intelligence is key, including in relation to timing;
- Be specific about your offer, how you can deliver it and what you want in return;
- Be confident enough to be flexible and perhaps adapt your deal positioning;
- Remember, "No" does not mean give up, rather it can be a reason to pivot, amend, and refresh; and
- **Always seek ethical, win-win deals—this does not mean surrender and never give anything for free.**

Deal-closing capabilities are innate abilities and, as you will now have seen, the premise of this book is that it is not difficult to develop, enhance, and expand these life skills provided you follow some simple steps as set out in the seven P approach to successful business deal execution:

1. **Principles**—*some deal-closing fundamentals.*
2. **Planning**—*if you fail to plan you plan to fail.*
3. **Power**—*the power balance is pivotal to the deal.*
4. **Players**—*who is who on both sides of the deal.*
5. **Performance**—*deal performance is all.*
6. **Putting It All to Bed**—*the deal close is critical.*
7. **Pay-Out or Post-Mortem**—*win or lose, learn for the next time.*

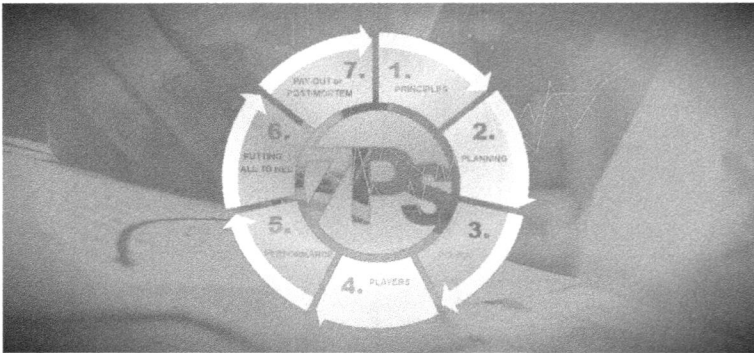

Simon writes, speaks, and mentors extensively on the subjects of deal-closing, strategy, business and leadership and can be contacted at simon@gcmadvisory.com or through simon@expertdealcloser.com for any related relevant requests.

Annex 1

Gender Balance and Its Importance in Negotiating Business Deals.
—Simon Haigh and Justin Caffrey

Reproduced with permission of Globelawandbusiness.com—2018

Introduction to Negotiation and Deal-Making

Deals are pivotal to business growth and are being struck all the time—2017 saw $3 trillion worth of merger and acquisition activity for the third year running, extending an unprecedented wave of deal making. The last few years have seen records set for global corporate deals. Record low interest rates in Western economies have helped to fuel a large part of this deal activity as companies have taken advantage of "cheap money" to buy, or merge with, competitors as a way to spur growth.

Negotiating skills are essential components of the successful deal-closer's armoury. *The Cambridge Dictionary Online* defines negotiation as: "To have formal discussions with someone in order to reach an agreement with them," and the *Cambridge Business English Dictionary* defines deal-making as: "The activity of making business agreements or arrangements."

Negotiation and deal-making are as much, if not more, about human behavior as they are about the facts, processes and systems used, or engaged in, during a deal process. We are consciously and subconsciously influenced by what we see and hear on the other side of the deal table. An accomplished negotiator or deal-maker needs experience, intuition, good communication skills, empathy and a strategic, flexible mindset.

The ability to negotiate deals successfully requires honed interpersonal skills for maximum success. With these skills, an accomplished deal negotiator can confidently ask for the outcome he or she is looking for, provided of course it is within reasonably achievable parameters. Armed with the skills of an accomplished negotiator, and provided the deal-maker communicates in an effective, meaningful and authentic way, he or she should not be afraid to ask for what they want in a deal.

To varying degrees, and at different times, we all strike deals in business, both internally for ourselves or on behalf of others, and externally on behalf of the organization for which we work. Every person or organization engages in deal-making at some point. From as far back as our childhood, we possessed the innate ability to get what we want through selling and negotiating and other means—remember when you used to stamp your feet to make sure you got your own way! We are born with an instinct for deal-making. Some people retain that deal-making instinct and develop it as they age, while others lose it for many reasons, such as social conditioning or lack of practice. Therefore, many of us are poorer at deal-making and thus miss out on better outcomes (see Simon Haigh, *Deal-making for Corporate Growth—The 7P Approach to Successful Business Deal Execution* [Dublin: Oak Tree Press 2016]).

Why Are Women Under-Represented in Negotiating Business Deals?

Good communication and positioning are critical for accomplished negotiation and deal-making. Gender balance optimization, balancing "feminine" collaborative and emotion-led communication-based attributes with "masculine" forthright, hierarchical and outcome-based attributes, is essential for accomplished, more sustainable, business deal negotiation. However, notwithstanding that we are all born with an instinct for negotiating deals, there is a deficit in utilizing these more feminine attributes where business deals are being negotiated.

Women are of course involved in negotiating business deals at all levels but, generally speaking, particularly at the higher echelons in organizations, they tend to be significantly underrepresented, both in terms of numbers and in terms of comparatively successful negotiation outcomes. This is despite the fact that women are well equipped for effective deal negotiation. As Edinburgh-based Gill Carrie, who has 38 years' experience in business and education with major organizations, companies and brands and has styled an empowering and inspirational "people experience" and won an Investors in People Award puts it: "Women are natural at deal-making, with a holistic approach whilst not necessarily seeing themselves as a 'deal-maker'—which, after all, is only a 'label' for an everyday process."

Historically, the key representatives of, and within, the state including law, politics, the military and the church have traditionally been masculine orientated. The women's suffrage movement, which commenced in the late 19th century, of course accelerated the feminine voice in society. The MeToo movement is also going a significant way to highlighting the strength of the feminine voice and its importance in balancing the masculine and feminine. But, despite societal progress, the United Kingdom has just concluded the Gender Pay Gap Review and the unequal male to female pay results have attracted a media storm. Women are still underrepresented, particularly at higher levels, including at board level, in professions, and at the negotiation and deal-making table. Centuries of male dominance is, and will, it seems, continue to take time to truly balance out. Nowhere is this perhaps more so than in business and in the realm of negotiating internal and external business deals.

Second generation gender bias, whereby the patterns of behavior that are traditionally more associated with men, such as aggression and hierarchical thinking and which are usually looked upon unfavorably in women, still pervades in the business arena. This in turn often results in women being underrepresented in negotiating business deals. Second-generation bias obviously holds women back. The insidious nature of this bias manifests itself in women becoming criticized, explicitly or more usually indirectly, for unnecessarily contravening the social norms of traditional female behavior—women often feel that they should not "ask for too much."

We tend to respond more positively toward successful men than successful women. Women often find it hard to succeed in this environment. Career-wise, women tend to negotiate less for themselves than women who negotiate on behalf of someone else regardless of who they are negotiating for. In anticipating prevailing biases, women tend to be bashful in fully seeking what they deserve from negotiations given their fear of being unduly criticized for being too "masculine" (aggressive, dominant, and arrogant) and insufficiently feminine (accommodating, protective, sensitive, communal, collaborative, and cooperative).

Other general biases pervade organizations and society as a whole about when, and on what basis, it is appropriate for women to exercise decision-making authority. Also, we have to face the fact that given the human tendency to gravitate to our own kind, senior men tend, on many occasions, to gravitate toward favoring other men when promotion and similar opportunities arise. Given that men have historically dominated the business world, it is perhaps not surprising that women generally have fewer, and less developed, support networks in place to overcome prevailing biases that, in turn, prevent them from being as dominant in negotiation business deals.

Why Is It Important to Increase the Representation of Women and the Feminine in Business Deal Negotiation?

Organizations exist through the combined sum total of the value of their people and the resultant power generates the fuel for the forward propulsion of the organization and its growth. Success is optimized when the whole company feels like it has a purpose. For an organization to really thrive, its entire people, provided they are the right people for the organization in question, need to feel empowered and effectively engaged—not ignored or under-utilized.

Both men and women are comprised, to varying degrees, of the masculine and feminine attributes. Women can be strong and aggressive and men can be gentle and compassionate. By operating through one predominant side of the gender equation, organizations are not optimizing their capabilities, thereby risking the success of the organization and the health, wellbeing and potential of employees. This authentic balance of both gender attributes promotes an environment of adaptability and growth while also being its own driver of diversity and equality. Such gender balance in turn is optimal for most effective business deal negotiation and therefore organizational growth. As Elaine Carroll, director and founder of the All-Ireland Business Summit and Business All-Stars Programme, observes:

> *Being able to look at the different perceptual positions in deal-making is like having secret ammunition. By having greater gender balance the ability to negotiate under the understanding of perceptual positions is the jewel in the crown and a real advantage.*

There is a tendency to think that a deal-closer must win and the other side must lose. If the only thing being negotiated is money, then yes, in that circumstance, a deal can be that straightforward. But we have very rarely been part of a deal scenario where money is the only factor at play. However, the goal of creating a good deal for both parties through mutual value satisfaction is not only possible, but also the only really sustainable way to do business.

Accordingly, we would argue that we are missing the point in perpetuating the masculine dominance in business deal negotiation and that the prism of deal-making should, in any event, be pivoted away from the traditional predominantly masculine attributes toward a balanced, masculine–feminine approach for more optimal outcomes. We are advocating for a more balanced internal and external business deal negotiation landscape. We are also arguing for greater female inclusion and greater engagement by both men and women with greater emphasis on feminine negotiation skills of "emotional intelligence, collaboration and sharpened listening" and a step away from the old-world binary outcomes.

What Can We Do to Increase the Representation of Women and the Feminine in Business Deal Negotiation?

As we have seen, we all negotiate deals in business, both internally for ourselves or on behalf of others, and externally on behalf of the organization. For the feminine voice in us all to truly be given the space and tools to be as successfully represented in business deal negotiation, organizations need to create and maintain an environment that allows for balance of the masculine and feminine in an open, authentic, collaborative and inclusive way. As such, we would suggest that organizations, and indeed all of us within organizations, could do a number of things to increase the true and effective representation of women and the feminine in effective business deal negotiation.

Develop Suitable Organizational Policies with Objective Measures

Organizations should, of course, be vigilant for gender bias in their recruitment, development and promotions policies, procedures, and processes. They should also seek to reinforce the positive positioning of accomplished female deal negotiators by matching them with senior executive mentors/

sponsors. Without this structured support in place, the immense power of prevailing biases will usually prevent the feminine from advancing as far as it should. Organizations should play their part in correcting the current biases and gender stereotypes by developing and enforcing policies, procedures, and processes through objective performance measures. In so doing, it is really important to constantly examine the organization's culture for hints of bias, gender stereotype nuances and ensuring gender-neutral practices are fully entrenched. Elaine Carroll makes the point that:

> *Supporting the role of females throughout their career paths through instituting meaningful organizational policies with reinforcing measurements is a more sustainable solution than quotas.*

Educate on, and Self-Check, Biases

We all, men and women, need to reflect on our own biases in terms of viewing aggressive women, or indeed women as a whole, as being unsuitable for deal-negotiation success. Also, when women recognize the extensive nature of second-generation bias, they are usually better armed to navigate more permanent positive results in a more confident manner.

Create a Safe Place for Sharing and Communicating

The underrepresentation of women in senior business positions only serves to reinforce the second generation and other biases and, as a consequence, the unfortunate status quo. Given the numerous layers of "bias glass-ceilings" that women face in business and, as a result, given the relative lack of senior women in business and deal-negotiation roles, a safe place for sharing, communicating, challenging, learning and innovating is to be encouraged. As Gill Carrie observes:

> *It is so fundamentally important that we all develop the confidence to bring our personal style to any negotiation process to enhance the deal-making experience for all involved. We need to balance the deal-making process with our own personal style. To help facilitate this, we all need to take ownership and create a healthy space within environments where it is safe to express, irrespective of gender.*

It is, in turn, really important to frame these rebalancing activities in terms of leadership development for all, rather than as a perception recalibration exercise. Organizations should build sharing and learning communities in which women can safely discuss their situations, compare experiences and support each other in their progress.

Provide Impactful Deal-Making Skills-Building and Mentoring Programmes

While we might all be born with an instinct for negotiating deals, providing impactful negotiation and deal-making training that provides the impetus for effective gender-neutral skills enhancement is essential. In addition, providing mentoring programmes to women to ensure that they are aware of promotion opportunities or chances to shine in the organization is very important.

Ensure that the Organization Audits and Seeks to Constantly Improve Its Full Deal and Negotiation Gender Representation Activities

Organizations can do this in a number of meaningful ways, from constantly reviewing their programmes to reflecting on who was engaged in which roles during the course of the review period. They can then reflect upon who was engaged, how male and female candidates were each communicated with and in return how they communicated back to the organization and to one another.

Focus on the Importance of Power in Deal Negotiation

A deal negotiator's relative power directly impacts his or her ability to execute deals. In fact, relative power is one of the most important factors that can determine the outcome of a deal.

Deal power is a frame of mind and can be developed. There is no formula for what a deal negotiator should open a deal with. Instead, he or she must consider and balance many issues, such as relationships, where the organization in question stands business-wise, who is in the deal room, and so on. In our experience, it will soon become clear if the deal negotiator has not been ambitious enough—mainly from the speed at which the other side accepts his or her first proposal. Therefore, it is important to open as ambitiously as possible, though of course being mindful of cultural differences in the way the negotiation opening is framed. Encouraging women to feel more powerful in their relative power results in their making more aggressive initial offers and then in negotiating better deal outcomes than women who remain subdued by the prevailing societal biases.

Can Accessing Feminine Empathy and Emotional Intelligence Offer a Potential Edge in Any Business Deal Negotiation?

Pursuing a win-win value approach to deal-making requires emotional intelligence, listening skills and ultimately patience, while at the same time parking ego in reception. The to-and-fro of a successful deal is hinged upon both parties getting what they want from it. Letting the other side know what you want and, at the same time, letting the other side be under the impression they can also get what they want in return, is essential. Listening to counterproposals and being flexible during the entire process is also critically important. A good deal negotiator employs carefully selected words and uses smart gestures. He or she also actively listens to the words used by the other side, while being alert to their subtle signs, gestures and other clues. It is important that you concentrate as fully as you can on how you come across, what you are saying, what you are not saying and your body language.

To maximize our deal-negotiating potential, we can no longer allow brash male egos to control businesses, economies or countries. As Elaine Carroll puts it:

> *The heightened sense of emotional intelligence which females bring to the table offers a cutting edge when it comes to deal-making. Having said that, raising awareness and educating males more in the area of emotional intelligence would also offer great benefits and advantages.*

All of the best outcomes in life come through negotiation and most of the best negotiation skills come from instinct. Many of these instincts of empathy and emotional intelligence lie within the feminine parts of us all. We all need to tap into the feminine within and certainly not deny women from celebrating their femininity while, like men, maximizing the balance through giving effect to the masculine in us all. We also need to create and maintain an environment that allows for this impeccable balance in natural energy, an environment of collaboration, openness, inclusiveness, and innovation.

Conclusion

Women are still largely underrepresented in the decision-making and therefore deal-making aspects of business, whether internally or externally. However, for an organization to really thrive and optimize its chances of having an optimal deal-making culture, all of its people need to be to be empowered. To encourage this, it is essential to create, and maintain, an environment that allows for balance of the masculine and feminine and one in which women can play their part as proficient deal-makers. More-over, it is essential that such an environment is one where the feminine in all of us is allowed to flourish. As Gill Carrie puts it:

It is empowering to be in a deal-making environment where gender is—or becomes—irrelevant. It is so important for an effective deal-making environment when there is no divide between the process and the feelings of the people in the process.

Regardless of an organization's strategy and planning, the success of any deal is reliant upon the people involved. An organization's choice of deal team is critically important as the shape of your team has a dramatic impact on your power. The right deal team members can enhance the knowledge, credibility, authority and perception of your team. So, who to include, who to leave out, roles and reporting methods are extremely important. If you are not optimizing the gender balance in your deal team you are not moving in the right direction and are unlikely to maximise the opportunities that are presented to you as society evolves. You should do all you can to ensure gender balance to enable successfully negotiated business deals.

Annex 2

Generation Entrepreni and the Emergence of New Business and Deal-Making Paradigms.

—Simon Haigh

Abstract

There is growing discussion about how generation Y (also known as millennials) and generation Z, whom the author collectively describes as "Generation Entrepreni," is changing the business landscape through their behavioral attributes. Is it also a coincidence that these same attributes happen to be aligned with good deal-making behaviors? This article provides an insight into this fascinating discussion. It is written in an accessible, easy-to-read, no-nonsense style and should be of interest to company executives, sales managers, and self-employed businesspeople. In fact, anyone who needs to make a deal.

Keywords

Business; deal-closing; deal-making; deals; entrepreneurs; negotiation

Introduction

To varying degrees, and at different times, we all strike deals (agreements or similar economic arrangements) in business and in other aspects of our lives. Every person or organization engages in deal-making at some point, regardless of whether they are aware of it or not. We possess the innate ability to get what we want through selling, negotiating, and other means—remember when you used to stamp your feet to make sure you got your own way? As I state in my e-book *Deal-Making for Corporate Growth—the 7P Approach to Successful Deal Execution*:

We are born with an instinct for deal-making. Some people retain that deal-making instinct and develop it as they age, while others lose it for many reasons such as social conditioning or lack of practice. And so, many of us are poorer at deal-making and thus miss out on better outcomes.

The nature of deal-making has undergone some paradigm shifts in keeping with the emergence of new generation of companies such as Uber, Classpass, Airbnb, Deliveroo, Netflix, Wework, Tripadvisor, and Trov. Minimal click purchasing, rapid delivery, real-time order status updates, and online feedbacks and reviews are becoming the new modern norms. How many people nowadays book restaurants and accommodation online without first checking prior online reviews?

Generation Y (or millennials) are identified as those who were born from the 1980s to the late 1990s/early 2000s, and generation Z as those who were born from the late 1990s/early 2000s (of which, see Lufkin [February 28, 2018]). I describe these two groups together as Generation Entrepreni, and ask to what extent, if at all, the behavioral attributes of Generation Entrepreni are shaping these shifts in the nature of deal-making?

The concept of younger generations influencing the way organizations conduct themselves is not new. For example, Jack Welch, while chief executive of General Electric in 1999, requested 500 of his key managers to pair up with younger workers to be "reverse mentored" in learning how to use the Internet most effectively.

Consumer, technology, and innovation trends are heavily influenced and/or driven by the tastes, consumption, and social media influencing patterns of younger generations. The influence of social media on brands together with growing technology use is contributing to changing the business landscape. Having grown up online, in an instantaneous "tweet world" of influencing, rapid feedbacks, and constant technology iterations and versions, Generation Entrepreni contributes to informing, shaping, and driving efficient, connected, and "always-on" business.

According to a survey of the current, and future, impact of millennials on M&A strategy at the annual Ernst and Young Deal Economy Conference—Predictions and Perspectives for 2017, "The rise of social media is also making it easier to launch and scale and start-up company—particularly in the consumer space." The increasing ease in accessing business establishment tools, such as incorporator.com.au and crowd funding, is also making it easier for Generation Entrepreni to get more directly involved in business.

Are these changes in business paradigms, driven largely by the behavioral attitudes of Generation Entrepreni, which in turn has been informed by the rapid, high-speed, networked environment in which they were raised, also reflected in their deal-making attributes?

Good Deal-Making Requires Flexible and Adaptable Deal Strategies

Business is unpredictable, not least as macro-and microeconomic factors are always changing. Deal-making in business is even more unpredictable, as it has its own particular set of obstacles, difficulties, and surprises that invariably arise: Factors such as ego, dubious business ethics, corrupt practices, a "head in the sand" mentality, anger, greed, and so on add extra layers of uncertainty to the business mix.

Many things can go wrong in a deal-making journey, such as derailing tactics from the other side, unhelpful egos among the stakeholders, internal or external blockages, or simply that the business environment changes during the deal-making process.

Being flexible in following a deal-making strategy and constantly monitoring and analyzing risk parameters are important ingredients for ensuring successful deal-making for corporate growth. In addition to being flexible, a good deal-maker also needs to be open to change and to learn from successes and mistakes in prior deals.

Generation Entrepreni has a predisposition to being flexible and nimble, driven largely by the instant social media world and constant technology changes. Possibly because it has grown up in the more transient, higher turnover "gig economy," Generation Entrepreni is also open to taking chances, and is adaptable and not afraid of failing in the process. The fact that generation Z, in particular, has grown up during the recent global recession has influenced its desire to be driven, but not at all costs. These are all deal-making positives.

Good Deal-Making Requires Good Negotiating Skills

The Cambridge Dictionary Online (n.d.) defines negotiating as: "To have formal discussions with someone in order to reach an agreement with them."

The ability to negotiate successfully requires honed interpersonal skills for maximum success. An accomplished negotiator can confidently ask for the outcome he/she is looking for, provided, of course, it is within reasonably achievable parameters. Armed with the skills of an accomplished negotiator, and provided he/she communicates in an effective, meaningful, and authentic way, a good deal-maker should not be afraid to ask for what he/she wants in a deal. Not least given the way that it is educated to challenge ideas, Generation Entrepreni tends not to be lacking in self-confidence, with a "can do" approach to doing things. With these skills, Generation Entrepreni should be generally well armed for negotiation. However, given that Generation Entrepreni has been brought up in a world of participation trophies and encouragement, it remains to be seen whether this might affect its resilience when it comes to longer, more complex, drawn out negotiations.

Deal Priorities and Values

As part of the deal-maker's planning and preparation phase, it is essential to decide his/her key issues and priorities, for example, what his/her opening position and bottom line need to be established and how and when to make the first move. Only then can the deal-maker realistically prepare his/her arguments and proposals. That said, he/she should resist the temptation of getting so fixated on achieving one issue that he/she loses sight of the relative, or potential, importance of other issues at play.

Deal-making requires an appreciation of what is important now, plus the ability to predict what will be important down the line and to balance the two. This requires a proactive, observant approach to deal-making. Given that Generation Entrepreni has, through its endless access to online information sources, had ample opportunity to watch, monitor, discuss, and learn from the failings of prior generations would suggest that it is well placed to take an informed and measured view in deal-making circumstances.

In deal-making, it is essential not to rush the first step of identifying and prioritizing all relevant issues. There are essentially two types of issues at play:

- **Primary issues**: Including location, size of deal, price, and so on;
- **Secondary issues**: The "nice to haves" but not essentials.

Once the primary and secondary issues have been worked out, the deal-maker is ready to enter what I have called the "deal zone."

To define the deal zone, it is necessary to research, prepare, and stress test the following positions (in order) for each of all primary (and some secondary) issues:

- **Likely outcome**: This is the deal-maker's realistic target to achieve;
- **Bottom line**: This is the deal-maker's absolute worst-case position at which he/she will walk away from the deal;
- **Opening position**: This is the best possible position the deal-maker thinks he/she might achieve.

The key outcome of defining the deal zone is to enable the deal-maker to eventually land somewhere between his/her opening and likely outcomes.

Developing the deal zone is really about determining how each side values the issues at play and identifying the zone in which a potential deal is possible. That zone should be a flexible win-win one. In referencing values in deal-making, as a rule, Generation Entrepreni is motivated by a sense of purpose, which often transcends traditional, more baby-boomer/gen X concepts of winning at all costs. A higher meaning than pure monetary reward, work-life balance and quality of life, is often a motivator for Generation Entrepreni. As such, the goal of creating a good deal for both parties through mutual value satisfaction is not only possible, but also the only really sustainable way to do business and one that Generation Entrepreni should be well suited to achieve.

It Is Important to Ask the Right Questions to Get the Right Answers

The use of direct questions is the time-honored way of gathering information from people willing to share it, but the questioning needs to be done in a careful, measured, thoughtful way. Face-to-face questioning also gives a deal-maker the invaluable opportunity to pick up on the hints, gestures, suggestions, and other subtleties that accompany the response. After all, the whole point of asking questions is to help the deal-maker explore and frame his/her "deal zone" for the deal and, in the process, to find out what the other side needs and wants. Generation Entrepreni likes to learn and is not afraid of asking questions and seeking opportunity through interaction, so is arguably well placed to ask the right questions to get the right answers.

Information and Knowledge Enhance Deal-Making Power

Careful planning allows the deal-maker to frame his/her preparations for maximum effect and maximum deal power, highlighting potential deal strengths and weaknesses and providing him/her with the ability to fix any holes in his/her position. Good deal-makers do not cut corners in their planning. As a first step, they conduct a comprehensive assessment of relative power between both sides. Relative power directly impacts the dealmaker's ability to execute deals. In fact, relative power is one of the most important factors that can determine the outcome of a deal.

Deal power is a frame of mind and can be developed. Even if initially it looks like there is a significant imbalance of power between both sides, by being smart, diligent, and measured, a good deal-maker can readjust that imbalance, for example, by moving the discussion away from price to quality or some other emotive subject.

Power is not static. It usually ebbs and flows during a deal and can change sides very quickly. Whether he/she likes it or not, a deal-maker's power is always influenced by his/her credibility, legitimacy, knowledge through information, authority, appearance, and influence. Perception is an extremely powerful power source in deal-making: Perceived power can be as powerful as actual power. Generation Entrepreni and particularly generation Z, appears to be particularly adept at managing perception, and even influencing others through self-brand projection on social media platforms in particular suggests that it is as well placed as any generation, and probably more so, from a perceived power perspective.

It is important for a good deal-maker to focus on building the appearance (or at least the perception) of his/her own power.

In a corporate environment, recognized types of power include:

Personal Organizational Power

This is based on a person's position within the organization's hierarchy. Generation Entrepreni tends to enjoy working and thrives in a collaborative environment. It prefers to foster less-hierarchical, closer, diverse structures within organizations where information tends to be freer flowing, which, as a rule, tends to bolster its personal organizational power. As Ronen Gafni and Simcha Gluck (2014) put it:

> *Knowing that they can win, and win faster through others, New Entrepreneurz always seek collaboration. Sharing platforms, creating joint ventures and smartnerships, and opting to expand the pie for everyone makes each action reverberate with power.*

Resources Power

This is comprised of the breadth and depth of resources at a person's disposal. Technology clearly plays an ever-increasingly important capital aspect within business. Generation Entrepreni has grown up with technology solutions and social media and its mastery of the opportunities that such digital platforms can deliver to them brings them a potential significant advantage.

Technology and the associated increased access to precedent information for informed decision making can open up the market, reduce the power gap between parties, reduce costs by cutting out expensive middlemen, and increase the speed, efficiency, and effectiveness of the deal-closing process. Clearly, Generation Entrepreni is best placed to avail of the benefits of technology usage in deal-making. Digital dexterity is second nature to Generation Entrepreni, and it is availing of the full suite of technology benefits to start up, run, and publicize business ventures. Technology itself is reinforcing the power of those who can master it best.

Shared History Power

This is based on insights from prior interactions with the other party. Generally speaking, the more the deal-maker knows about the other side, the more he/she can plan and prepare his/her way to an effective strategy against them to optimize their deal (though, of course, this power is available to both parties).

Informational Power

This is where a person has access to important or valuable information. Information can clearly build the deal-maker's power. It follows that, as information underpins knowledge, converting information into knowledge produces the opportunity for even more power. Understanding the relevance and importance of information, and how it can be leveraged, can assist in building the deal-maker's power. The more a deal-maker knows about what is unfolding, the more he/she can reliably assess your position, develop his/her strategy, and then plan how to best execute the deal. Not only is information relevant to the interparty dynamics, but good information management skills are also essential in corporate deals to avoid wrong decisions. Given Generation Entrepreni tends to embrace collaboration and flatter organizational structures and, therefore, two-way free-flowing information sharing, it is again well disposed to bolster its informational power balance.

Networks and Relationships Increase Your Information Base and Deal Power

The closer the deal-maker gets to knowing the intentions, desires, and assumptions of the other side in a deal, the more likely he/she is to ultimately getting what he/she wants from the deal. So, using networks and relationships is a very important additional way for deal-makers to gather the all-important information they need, which then enhances their knowledge and ultimately their power. This is particularly the case if the network or relationship connects the deal-maker to the key decision maker(s) on the other side. The Pew Research Center—Fenn (2009) has affirmed that Generation Entrepreni is history's first "always connected" generation and so its networks are geometrically increased as a result. Whether these increased networks are always effective given that Generation Enterpreni does not operate in as communication nuanced face-to-face manner as compared to prior generations, is another question, however.

Good Communication Is Critical for Effective Deal-Making

The "to and fro" of a successful deal is hinged upon both parties getting what they want from it. Good communication is critical for good deal-making. Letting the other side know what the deal-maker wants and, at the same time, letting the other side be under the impression they can also get what they want in return is essential. Listening to counterproposals, and being flexible during the entire process, is also critically important.

A good deal-maker employs carefully selected words and uses smart gestures. He/she also actively listens to the words used by the other side, while being very alert to their subtle signs, gestures, and other clues. But, be aware that, even with language itself (let alone nonverbal communication), there are vast differences between cultures that give different meanings to certain words such as "reasonable" or "progress."

The fact that Generation Entrepreni appears to be more culturally, sexually, and racially tolerant than its predecessors in its attitudes, preferences, and communication manners certainly appears to auger well for a "culturally competent," collaborative, and innovative deal-making communication mindset.

Good Deal-Makers See the Bigger Picture

Despite the best efforts in putting a good deal on the table, the vagaries of deal-making mean that things can, and often do, go wrong. Not all deal discussions will result in a successful deal. Sometimes deadlock or dispute will arise.

Be aware that a "No" from the other side does not always mean that the deal is at an end. Too often parties walk away at this point, but many times in deal discussions I have heard "No" and yet I have seen a way forward. A good deal-maker will use "No" as a cue to reframe and try a new tactic. Be aware too that not consummating a deal does not always mean failure. It might even be the right outcome—perhaps there was not really a deal there. Given that Generation Entrepreni has grown up in a fast-moving, ever-changing world, it is perhaps well oriented to being comfortable with a "No" approach to business. It remains to be seen whether this provides an impetus for Generation Entrepreni to adopt more sustainable business and deal-making practices than prior generations.

Conclusion

There is little doubt that Generation Entrepreni is impacting the business landscape, for example, in the technology, innovative, collaborative solutions, and consumer markets. This is perhaps not surprising given that Generation Entrepreni has grown up online, in an instantaneous, digital "tweet world" of rapid feedbacks and constant technology iterations. The environment in which Generation Entrepreni has been raised, of rapid, high-speed, networked communications, has clearly shaped their behavioral attributes and so also their business choices.

It also happens to be the case that Generation Entrepreni appears to possess many of the attributes required for good deal-making. Generation Entrepreni has a predisposition for being nimble, is adaptable to change, and is flexible, with a self-reliant, self-confident "can do, give it a go" attitude. It is not afraid of taking chances and perhaps failing in the process. Its sense of purpose, collaborative spirit, increased tolerance, and accommodation for freer flowing information sharing are all positive factors in Generation Entrepreni's deal-making capabilities. Does this new body of Generation Entrepreni attributes represent evidence of a new deal-making paradigm, being a generation of accomplished deal-makers uniquely placed to shape the business and deal-making landscape? Alternatively, is it just a manifestation of convenient coincidence, shaped by the environment in which Generation Entrepreni has developed? What is clear is that, as with all suppositions, the answer will lie in the judgment of future generations.

Annex 3

EXPERTDEALCLOSER.COM
in association with GCM

Coaching Questionnaire

New Pathways to Increase Your Deal Success Ratios

Name: _____

Please enter below your top 5 requirements based upon the prompts below, in order of priority.
We will review these in the first coaching session and then drill down into the specific priorities.

1. _____
2. _____
3. _____
4. _____
5. _____

Please return to info@gcmadvisory.com.

What Do You Need Our Help With?

Deal Opportunity Stage

- Is your deal team process too slow? Does it need to be accelerated to enhance profitable returns?
- Do you struggle to develop, and maintain, a scalable process that drives consistent value for both sides?

Deal Lead Generation Stage

- Is your deal team process too slow? Does it need to be accelerated to enhance profitable returns?
- Do you struggle to develop, and maintain, a scalable process that drives consistent value for both sides?

Deal Tender/Proposal Generation Stage

- Is your deal team process too slow? Does it need to be accelerated to enhance profitable returns?
- Do you struggle to develop, and maintain, a scalable process that drives consistent value for both sides?

Deal Process Stage: Principles

- Is your deal team process too slow? Does it need to be accelerated to enhance profitable returns?
- Do you struggle to develop, and maintain, a scalable process that drives consistent value for both sides?
- Have you created a clear and simple strategy?
- Have you thought about the value requirements of the other side rather than price?
- Have you used value propositions in a sale and sought out the motives of the other side in a negotiation?
- Do you have sufficient negotiation capabilities and confidence?
- Have you thought through the deal requirements of the other side to foresee their must haves and objections to enable you to better understand their value drivers?
- Do you know, understand and have systems in place to deal with the best and worst case scenarios as the deal progresses?
- Have you considered alternative pathways to deal-making success including BATNA?
- Do you have a process in place to counter derailing tactics from the other side?

EXPERTDEALCLOSER.COM
in association with GCM

Coaching Questionnaire

Deal Process Stage: Planning

- Is your deal team process too slow? Does it need to be accelerated to enhance profitable returns?
- Do you struggle to develop, and maintain, a scalable process that drives consistent value for both sides?
- Have you thoroughly planned your strategy with risk analysis in place?
- Have you asked the right questions to get the right answers?
- Have you used simple, common, uncluttered language and sufficiently clarified issues?
- Have you asked closed questions?
- Have you given the other side time to answer?
- Have you used face-to-face questioning to pick up on hints, gestures, suggestions and other subtleties?
- Are you sure the other side is sure which information is important or relevant to provide- it is your responsibility to do so?
- Have you done all necessary to ensure the other side trusts you?
- Have you probed the information provided by the other side and conducted due diligence to ensure you get as close as possible to their true intentions?
- Have you considered what could go right and wrong throughout the process?
- Have you determined what information you have and what is missing?
- Have you set, and recorded, your deal parameters?
- Are you clear on who you are dealing with?
- Are you clear on the basis for the deal?
- Are you sure you know what the main issues are?
- Have you considered the possible outcomes?
- Have you used the right deal location and dynamics to fit cultural and other dynamics?
- Have you identified the primary (e.g. location, size of deal, price etc.) and secondary (nice to haves) issues at play?
- Have you distinguished between personal wants and business needs?
- Have you developed your deal zone- likely outcome, bottom line and opening position?

Deal Process Stage: Preparing for Power

- Is your deal team process too slow? Does it need to be accelerated to enhance profitable returns?
- Do you struggle to develop, and maintain, a scalable process that drives consistent value for both sides?
- Have you fully considered cultural issues and been culturally astute?
- Have you used information and knowledge to enhance your power?
- Are you sure you have the right information?
- Have you listened deeply and used silence strategically?
- Are you sure you have used active listening skills- been fully present and engaged in the communication, with both body and mind actively involved?
- Have you optimized your networks and relationships to increase your information base and deal power?
- Have you built relationships based upon mutual trust?
- Is your judgment skewed by getting too close to the other side?
- Have you conducted a comprehensive assessment of relative power between the sides?
- How do you project your credibility, legitimacy, knowledge, authority, appearance and influence?
- Have you built the appearance, or at least perception, of your power through a SWOT, incentives, persuasion, networks, contacts and relationships or cultural awareness?
- Have you used time-outs at the right time in the deal process to give you more power?
- Have you used an agenda to control the discussion?
- Have you set, and circulated, the agenda in advance of the deal meeting?
- Have you used deal sheets to reinforce your power?
- Have you constantly made your own notes of the deal discussions during the deal process?
- Have you leveraged your personal organisational power based upon your position within your organization's hierarchy?
- Have you leveraged your resources power (what resources are at your disposal)?
- Have you leveraged your shared history power based upon insights from prior interactions with the other side?

EXPERTDEALCLOSER.COM

in association with GCM

Coaching Questionnaire

Deal Process Stage: Players

- Is your deal team process too slow? Does it need to be accelerated to enhance profitable returns?
- Do you struggle to develop, and maintain, a scalable process that drives consistent value for both sides?
- Have you sufficiently identified both sides' core deal team roles including strategist, dealmaker, interpreter, coordinator or implementer?
- Have you chosen your deal team carefully?
- Have you mapped out the key players on the other side of the table including their respective power, influence etc.?
- Are you sure you have identified the other side's motives, intentions, strengths and weaknesses?
- Do you have a strategy to determine who to include, who to leave out, roles and reporting methods?
- Do you have sub-optimised silos instead of a collaborative environment of asking and sharing?
- Have you been smart in your use of experts?
- Have you briefed your expert as fully and comprehensively as possible?

Deal Process Stage: Performance

- Is your deal team process too slow? Does it need to be accelerated to enhance profitable returns?
- Do you struggle to develop, and maintain, a scalable process that drives consistent value for both sides?
- Have you sufficiently rehearsed/reviewed your plan?
- Have you tested, substantiated and verified your arguments, assumptions and general direction?
- Have you rehearsed your close to draw out any last-minute problems, issues, previously unidentified motivations, opinions and anything else that could, at actual close, derail the deal?
- Have you been the first to propose?
- Have you maximized the three deal stages of offer, counter-offer and close?
- Have you done your due diligence and then let the other side know what you are prepared to offer them?
- Have you opened as ambitiously as possible?
- Have you been smart in framing your proposal?
- Have you been as concise as possible and presented your case in a logical, comprehensible sequential way?
- Have you introduced your proposal, broken down clearly what you are saying by using facts and resisted the temptation to offer opinion, tried to get closure by testing how the other side feels about each element of your proposal and ensured you opened the other side up as much as possible in terms of their thinking and direction. Have you repeated all the above?
- Have you stopped yourself from showing temper, defensiveness, irritability, confrontational style or impatience?
- Have you asked questions and adapted your proposals and the general direction of the deal based upon the responses?
- Have you recorded all detail through note taking and summarizing throughout?
- Have you used prudent communication/common language?
- Have you let the other side know what you want and, at the same time, let the other side be under the impression they can also get what they want in return?
- Have you used carefully selected words and used smart gestures?
- Are you influenced by the other side's appearance, race, age, gender and so on?
- Do you use tactics to prevent the other side from derailing you such as ignoring them, pre-empting them by way of advanced planning or calling them out for what they are?
- Have you concentrated as fully as you can on how you come across, what you are saying, what you are not saying and your body language?
- Have you used firm language and a deeper voice while looking comfortable, composed and authoritative, whilst being conscious of (and if necessary, addressing) your own movements?
- Have you used deadlines as a focusing tactic?
- Have you leveraged incentives to address the needs and wants of the other side?
- Have you determined whether it is right to close the deal or walk away?
- Have you efficiently determined what is causing the blockage and dealt with it comprehensively and quickly?
- Have you considered engaging a trusted third party such as a mediator to break the impasse?
- Have you considered tactics to get the deal back on track such as changing your deal team, making a new proposal, reframing your existing proposal or simply adjournment?
- Have you escalated the matter to your boss, altered your deal zone parameters, or called a cooling off period?

EXPERTDEALCLOSER.COM
in association with GCM

Coaching Questionnaire

Deal Process Stage: Putting it All to Bed

- Is your deal team process too slow? Does it need to be accelerated to enhance profitable returns?
- Do you struggle to develop, and maintain, a scalable process that drives consistent value for both sides?
- Have you checked that nothing has been left off the table?
- Have you used a checklist to ensure that there is nothing left to be discussed?
- Have you clarified mutual understanding?
- Have you used common language?
- Are you happy with where things are heading? Are all the members of the opposing team happy? Can you sense any dissent among them?
- Have you used closed questions where possible?
- Have you summarized the deal and compared where you have landed against your likely outcome?
- Have you ensured that the other side explicitly agrees that this is their understanding so as to minimize the possibility of any later conflict?
- Have you memorialized the deal through use of an MOU, letter of intent, heads of agreement or otherwise?
- Have you future-proofed your agreement by inserting performance KPIs, trigger points, service level agreements or otherwise?
- Have you ensured that the terms of the agreement are as concise, clear and unequivocal as possible?
- Have you ensured that you have led this end of the process rather than let the other side?
- Have you agreed on the implementation plan prior to execution?
- Have you put in place an internal stakeholder program to ensure their buy in to ease execution?
- Have you prepared for divorce – just in case?
- Do you struggle to close deals on time and on budget- slippage?

Deal Process Stage: Pay-out or Post-mortem

- Is your deal team process too slow? Does it need to be accelerated to enhance profitable returns?
- Do you struggle to develop, and maintain, a scalable process that drives consistent value for both sides?
- Have you measured your deal success-wise? Do you have systems in place to do so?
- Have you scheduled time immediately after the conclusion of a deal to systematically review the elements of the deal journey, to identify areas of improvement and to note newly introduced tactics that worked well and could be used again?
- Have you conducted a formal post-mortem on your deal journey?
- Do you have systems to monitor your deal-closing processes and learn from prior mistakes?

Annex 4

Expertdealcloser.com Personal Success Deal-closing Skills Program Summary

We can help:

- Increase revenues through effective **deal-closing**;
- Improve face to face and online **sales** results;
- Enhance business development through efficient **collaboration and communication**;
- Maximize business opportunities through **negotiation** excellence;
- Optimize business growth through an enhanced culture of **deal-making**.

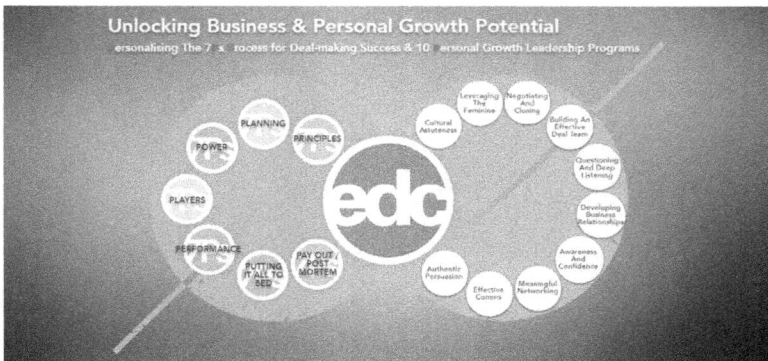

References

The Cambridge Business English Dictionary

Fisher, R., W.L. Ury, and B. Patton. 1991. "Introduced in their Seminal Book." In *Getting to Yes: Negotiating Agreement Without Giving*, 2nd ed. Penguin.

www.FT.com

https://www2.deloitte.com/uk/en/pages/financial-advisory/articles/future-of-the-deal.html

www.thefreedictionary.com

www. dictionary.cambridge.org

https://bloombergquint.com/business/2018/06/21/the-biggest-deal-boom-in-a-decade-will-only-get-bigger-heres-why

Globelawandbusiness.com

About the Author

Simon P. Haigh has a diverse 25-year international experience over three continents, five countries, a number of industries and roles including C-Suite legal, dealmaking, strategic, organizational transformation and commercial with Dell, BHP, Xilinx, NANA Development Corporation and leading global law firms.

Simon is an, author, entrepreneur, director, consultant, Marshall Goldsmith certified coach, keynote speaker, mentor, trained mediator and executive education unit lead and lecturer in Deal-Execution at Trinity College, Dublin, Ireland. Simon is author of Contract Law in an E-Commerce Age (Round-Hall Sweet and Maxwell 2001) and Dealmaking for Corporate Growth—the 7Ps of Successful Business Deal Execution—available on www.amazon.com (foreword by Marshall Goldsmith—international best-selling author of Triggers and What Got You Here Won't get You There).

Simon holds a BA (Hons) Law from Durham University, England, an MBA from Curtin University, Western Australia, Business Process Improvement Green and Yellow Belts and Applied Project Management qualifications. Simon is also a Graduate of the Australian Institute of Company Directors.

Simon has a fast growing international reputation for consummating major commercial deals, combining entrepreneurial capability with corporate and professional underpinning. He is founder and Managing Director of a global advisory firm GCM Advisory (www.gcmadvisory.com) and its sister business www.expertdealcloser.com. Simon is also Managing Director, Brand Finance Ireland, the leading global independent brand valuation agency. When he is not making deals, Simon mentors budding entrepreneurs in the art of dealmaking.

Simon is founder of www.expertdealcloser.com whose products include: Consulting, coaching, mentoring, and speaking
https://expertdealcloser.com/consulting-coaching-mentoring

Publications:
https://expertdealcloser.com/publications

Tools:
https://expertdealcloser.com/tools

Online and face-face training, workshops, and events:
https://expertdealcloser.com/training-workshops-events

Index

OTHER TITLES IN OUR SELLING AND SALES FORCE MANAGEMENT COLLECTION

- *Creating Effective Sales and Marketing Relationships* by Kenneth Le Meunier-FitzHugh and Leslie Caroline Le Meunier-FitzHugh
- *Lean Application in Sales: How a Sales Manager Applied Lean Tools to Sales Processes and Exceeded His Goals* by Jaideep Motwani and Rob Ptacek
- *Improving Sales and Marketing Collaboration: A Step-by-Step Guide* by Avinash Malshe and Wim Biemans
- *Key Account Management: Strategies to Leverage Information, Technology, and Relationships to Deliver Value to Large Customers* by Joel Le Bon and Carl Herman
- *Selling: The New Norm: Dynamic New Methods for a Competitive and Changing World* by Drew Stevens

Announcing the Business Expert Press Digital Library

Concise e-books business students need for classroom and research

This book can also be purchased in an e-book collection by your library as

- a one-time purchase,
- that is owned forever,
- allows for simultaneous readers,
- has no restrictions on printing, and
- can be downloaded as PDFs from within the library community.

Our digital library collections are a great solution to beat the rising cost of textbooks. E-books can be loaded into their course management systems or onto students' e-book readers.
The **Business Expert Press** digital libraries are very affordable, with no obligation to buy in future years. For more information, please visit **www.businessexpertpress.com/librarians**. To set up a trial in the United States, please email **sales@businessexpertpress.com**.